HOW TO M.
WEDDING S

In this Series

How to Apply for a Job
How to Apply to an Industrial Tribunal
How to Be a Freelance Journalist
How to Be a Freelance Sales Agent
How to Be a Freelance Secretary
How to Be a Local Councillor
How to Be an Effective School Governor
How to Become an Au Pair
How to Buy & Run a Shop
How to Buy & Run a Small Hotel
How to Choose a Private School
How to Claim State Benefits
How to Communicate at Work
How to Conduct Staff Appraisals
How to Counsel People at Work
How to Do Voluntary Work Abroad
How to Do Your Own Advertising
How to Do Your Own PR
How to Emigrate
How to Employ & Manage Staff
How to Enjoy Retirement
How to Find Temporary Work Abroad
How to Get a Job Abroad
How to Get a Job in America
How to Get a Job in Australia
How to Get a Job in Europe
How to Get a Job in France
How to Get a Job in Germany
How to Get a Job in Hotels & Catering
How to Get a Job in Travel & Tourism
How to Get into Films & TV
How to Get into Radio
How to Get That Job
How to Help Your Child at School
How to Invest in Stocks & Shares
How to Keep Business Accounts
How to Know Your Rights at Work
How to Know Your Rights: Students
How to Know Your Rights: Teachers
How to Live & Work in America
How to Live & Work in Australia
How to Live & Work in Belgium
How to Live & Work in France
How to Live & Work in Germany
How to Live & Work in Hong Kong
How to Live & Work in Italy
How to Live & Work in Japan
How to Live & Work in New Zealand
How to Live & Work in Portugal
How to Live & Work in Saudi Arabia
How to Live & Work in Spain
How to Live & Work in the Gulf

How to Lose Weight & Keep Fit
How to Make a Wedding Speech
How to Manage a Sales Team
How to Manage Budgets & Cash Flows
How to Manage Computers at Work
How to Manage People at Work
How to Manage Your Career
How to Master Book-Keeping
How to Master Business English
How to Master GCSE Accounts
How to Master Languages
How to Master Public Speaking
How to Pass Exams Without Anxiety
How to Pass That Interview
How to Plan a Wedding
How to Prepare Your Child for School
How to Publish a Book
How to Publish a Newsletter
How to Raise Business Finance
How to Raise Funds & Sponsorship
How to Rent & Buy Property in France
How to Rent & Buy Property in Italy
How to Retire Abroad
How to Return to Work
How to Run a Local Campaign
How to Run a Voluntary Group
How to Sell Your Business
How to Spend a Year Abroad
How to Start a Business from Home
How to Start a New Career
How to Start Word Processing
How to Start Your Own Business
How to Study Abroad
How to Study & Learn
How to Study & Live in Britain
How to Survive at College
How to Survive Divorce
How to Take Care of Your Heart
How to Teach Abroad
How to Travel Round the World
How to Understand Finance at Work
How to Use a Library
How to Work from Home
How to Work in an Office
How to Work with Dogs
How to Write a Press Release
How to Write a Report
How to Write an Assignment
How to Write an Essay
How to Write Business Letters
How to Write for Publication
How to Write for Television

Other titles in preparation

MAKE A
WEDDING SPEECH

Choosing the right words for every occasion

John Bowden

Second Edition

How To Books

'Ladies and Gentlemen, this is only the second time I've ever been a best man. I hope I did the job alright that time. The couple in question are at least still talking to me. Unfortunately, they're not actually talking to each other . . . but I'm sure that has absolutely nothing to do with me. Apparently Paula knew Piers had slept with her younger sister before I mentioned it in my speech. The fact that he had slept with her mother came as a surprise.'

(Hugh Grant in *Four Weddings and a Funeral*)

British Library Cataloguing in Publication Data
A catalogue record for this book is available from the British Library.

© Copyright 1994 and 1995 by John Bowden.

Published by How To Books Ltd, Plymbridge House, Estover Road, Plymouth PL6 7PZ, United Kingdom. Tel: Plymouth (01752) 735251/ 695745. Fax: (01752) 695699. Telex: 45635.

First edition 1994
Second edition (revised) 1995

Note: The material contained in this book is set out in good faith for general guidance and no liability can be accepted for loss or expense incurred as a result of relying in particular circumstances on statements made in this book. The law and regulations are complex and liable to change, and readers should check the current position with the relevant authorities before making personal arrangements.

Typeset by Concept Communications (Design & Print) Ltd, Crayford, Kent.
Printed and bound by The Cromwell Press, Broughton Gifford, Melksham, Wiltshire.

Contents

5

Preface

to the Second Edition

So you have been asked 'to say a few words' on the big day. The problem is we don't get much practice, do we? That's why this book will prove so useful to you. It will tell you how to prepare and deliver a unique and memorable little speech which even the most seasoned public speaker would be proud of. What's more, it's going to be fun!

Humour is a very important ingredient in any successful wedding speech, and I am therefore greatly indebted to the following professional funnymen and funnywomen who kindly took time out to tell me — and you — how they 'make 'em laugh':

Russ Abbot, Rowan Atkinson, Honor Blackman, Jim Bowen, Bob Carolgees, Jimmy Cricket, Paul Daniels, Lenny Henry, Roy Hudd, John Inman, Polly James, Joanna Lumley, Ruth Madoc, Walter Matthau, Leslie Phillips, Andrew Sachs, Richard Stilgoe, Mollie Sugden, Chris Tarrant and Richard Wilson.

This second edition is crammed with even more classics of humour and a host of fresh one-liners that would prove surefire hits in any wedding speech. You'll find something old, something new, plenty borrowed, but absolutely nothing blue!

There is also a revised and expanded chapter on coping with nerves. A speechmaker is a showman — a performer — an entertainer. And even the most experienced pro can suffer from a sudden attack of the collywobbles as he faces his audience. Discover the techniques and tricks of the trade that comedians use to control their nerves — and even turn them to their advantage.

A wedding speech is like a marriage — most successful when entered into with enthusiasm from both parties, in this case the speaker and the audience. Your audience is sure to be enthusiastic. Once you have read this book, you will be too.

John Bowden

7

1
Making a Wedding Speech

Recipe for a great wedding speech? No waffle and plenty of shortening. After a good meal and a drink or three, your audience will be in no mood for long, boring speeches. All they want is a few sincere and hopefully entertaining words. Two to five minutes (about 250 to 650 words) is plenty long enough at a wedding reception, and at an informal wedding party it can be even shorter. This book will help you decide exactly what to say to really make the most of those few minutes.

If you are going to make a wedding speech you should always remember these three little words:

KISS THE BRIDE

This will remind you of two vital things. Firstly, the word KISS will remind you to:

Keep
It
Short and
Simple.

We live in the age of the sound bite – people expect information to be presented concisely. Don't suffer from the illusion that you can make your speech immortal by making it everlasting. In the Bible, the story of the Creation is told in less than 400 words and the Ten Commandments are covered in less than 300. So I am sure you can say everything you need in less than 650. Size *does* matter. And no speech can be entirely bad if it's short enough.

Secondly, THE BRIDE will remind you that it is *her* big day. Don't spoil it by embarrassing her or by knocking the institution of marriage.

Remember: KISS THE BRIDE and you can't go far wrong!

Anyone called upon to make a speech must know how to do two

9

things: how to *prepare* it and how to *present* it. Let's begin with the preparation.

PREPARATION

Failing to prepare is preparing to fail.

Sir Winston Churchill once said he could prepare a two-hour speech in five minutes, but a five-minute speech would take him two hours. What he meant by that was that if you make a long speech you can afford to be quite wordy so you need only to think about the broad areas you want to cover; whereas if you make a short speech, every single word you use must be strictly relevant. Remember: no waffle and plenty of shortening.

Successful speech makers need to carefully PLAN what they are going to say. They must always consider their:

> **P**urpose
> **L**anguage
> **A**udience and
> **N**arrative.

Let's consider each of these in turn.

Purpose

The main purpose of a wedding speech is to propose a toast or to respond to one, or to do both. The usual sequence is:

- Speech 1: Proposal of a toast to the bride and groom.
- Speech 2: Response to the toast and then proposal of a second toast.
- Speech 3: Response to the second toast on behalf of the brides-maids.

Traditionally, the bride's father (or a close relative or family friend) makes the first speech; the bridegroom makes the second (making it clear that he is also speaking on behalf of his wife); and the best man makes the third. However, it is perfectly acceptable for other people to speak instead of or as well as these. It all depends on the particular circumstances and backgrounds of the newlyweds. We will consider this in much more detail in Chapter 7. At this stage all you need to bear in mind is that if you speak you must know your precise purpose. And it will be to propose a toast, to respond to a toast, or to do both.

Language

Forget about the rules of written English. You should use spoken not written English, so be yourself and speak in your natural voice. The best sort of wedding speech is presented in simple, chatty, everyday spoken English. Use language designed to be *said*, not to be *read*.

Audience

Any speaker must always remember the audience. Your task is simply to give them what they want and expect. And all they want and expect is a few well-chosen words of humour, and a few words of seriousness – all applied with liberal helpings of sentiment. But they deserve more than that; they deserve the best you can give them. You are lucky; most speakers first have to win over their audience. Your audience is already on your side. It is in a happy wedding day mood and it is willing you to succeed.

Narrative

So what are you going to say to them? Lewis Carroll's White Rabbit asked, 'Where shall I begin?' The reply he received was: 'Begin at the beginning and go on to the end, and then stop.'

It is the same for you: your speech should contain three sections – a great beginning, middle and end.

Beginning

Really grab your audience's attention from the word go with a great hook. Make them sit up and take notice. The best way to do this is to say something unexpected, funny, powerful or emotional, or to amaze them by telling them about some famous events that have occurred on this very day in years gone by.

Middle
This is the main body of the speech. Remember to give the audience what they want: a few sincere, optimistic and entertaining words. The bride's father's and the groom's speeches should include the right balance of humour and seriousness. The best man's should be by far the most lighthearted and should avoid anything serious. All three speeches might contain an anecdote; one or two jokes; a quotation; or perhaps some reference to the couple's names. It is important not to say too much. Quality is far more important than quantity. Leave them wanting more.

There are some subtle differences in the messages expected from the three main speakers, as follows:

Bride's father
This speech should contain some positive thoughts about the couple and about love and marriage in general. He could:

● Thank everyone for coming to celebrate his daughter's happy day.

● Say a few affectionate words about the bride and bridegroom.

● Talk of the happiness he and his wife have experienced in bringing up their daughter. What a treasure she has been to them.

● Relate one or two amusing or serious incidents from her childhood.

● Stress his positive feelings about his new son-in-law (and his parents) whom he welcomes to his family ('I am not losing a daughter; I am gaining a son').

● Offer some (possibly amusing) thoughts about love and what makes a happy marriage.

● Declare his confidence that the bride and groom will make all the effort needed and will not be found wanting.

Bridegroom
This is really a general thank you speech. He could:

● Say he is also speaking on behalf of the bride ('My wife and I. . .').

● Thank the bride's father for his kind remarks and good wishes, and also for laying on this reception.

- Thank both mothers for their help (whether they have or not).

- Thank the bride's parents for letting him marry their daughter and refer to anything they may have provided for the couple's future.

- Add a few affectionate words about his own parents, perhaps including, 'thank you for having me' or a reference to their kindness, care and attention during his boyhood.

- Acknowledge the invaluable services of the best man, and possibly also of the chief bridesmaid.

- Thank the guests for their presence – and for their presents.

- Tell everyone how lucky he is to marry such a wonderful bride, possibly relating a short, amusing episode involving their first meeting or engagement. He will dedicate himself to her happiness.

- Conclude with some complimentary words about the bridesmaids (calling them 'charming' or 'delightful' is much safer than calling them 'beautiful').

Best man
This is a response on behalf of all the attendants. Unlike the first two speakers, he should not say anything remotely serious or emotional. He could:

- Thank the bridegroom for the toast to the bridesmaids.

- Add a few complimentary comments of his own about them.

- Make a few light-hearted remarks about the bridegroom (positive remarks with absolutely no references to any past flames).

- Offer some sincere and complimentary thoughts about the groom and the bride.

- Congratulate the bridegroom on his good luck and wish the couple happiness for the future.

- Read the tele-messages (having first checked that they are suitable for public consumption), possibly making up the final one, claiming it came from some famous and long-dead person. ('And finally, here's one from Henry VIII. It says, "Congratulations, this is the happiest day of your lives – and good luck for your wedding tomorrow!"') Or perhaps from some TV character he knows they enjoy watching. ('And the last message comes from someone called Arfur Daley. It says: "Best wishes from all at the Winchester Club and from 'er indoors. The world is your lobster. Regards Arfur."')

End

A wedding speech is like a love affair. Any fool can start it, but to end it requires considerable skill. The film producer Sam Goldwyn once told a script writer: 'What we want is a story that starts with an earthquake and works its way up to a climax.' It's the same with your speech. Begin with a great hook, then say a few sincere and entertaining words which strike the right balance between seriousness and humour, and finally build up to a big finish. Try to end on a note of high emotion or with a witty, wise or uplifting and relevant little quotation or anecdote that will leave them gobsmacked. Aim for a verbal final round KO. People will remember that, regardless of what has preceded it in the previous rounds.

Whatever you do, don't let your speech end in an anticlimax. *Never* finish with:

- An apology for a poor speech.

- A whimper: 'Well I can't think of anything else. . .'; or 'Right, that's it. Thank you.')

- A long joke or story.

- A series of false endings. ('And finally, . . .; And finally, . . .; And finally, . . .'.)

- A reference to any new topic, such as an engagement. Remember this is the bride's day – and nobody else's.

And finally, where appropriate, don't forget to propose that toast.

Once you have thought very carefully about your PLAN (Purpose; Language; Audience; and Narrative), it is time to get a few of your thoughts down on paper. Start as early as possible. This will give you the chance to add things, take them out or rearrange them as the speech develops in your mind and on paper. Try to form links between the things you intend to say. In other words, make sure it flows.

Most people write out their draft speech in full. This is fine so long as you don't simply read it out on the big day. If you did you would lose all sense of contact with your audience and would appear nervous and insincere. You could just as well photocopy it and hand copies out.

It is far better to reduce your draft speech to perhaps half a dozen key-words, phrases or memory joggers, that you can glance at from time to time as you speak. By doing this you will be sure to cover everything you want to while at the same time appearing to be far more spontaneous and natural because you will be *speaking*, not *reading* a prepared speech. Here are some keywords and phrases that the bride's father could write on a small cue card to remind him of model speech 1 (which is written out in full in Chapter 7).

---

1   We cannot fully enjoy . . .

2   Karen – new chapter

3   Richard – knows where going

4   Housekeeping set

5   Same suit

6   Advice? Last word "sorry"

7   Health and happiness

But don't work too hard on your speech, especially if the wedding is still months away. Relax. Sleep on it. You really will get some of your best ideas that way. Putting your speech to the back of your mind will trigger the remarkable and usually untapped forces within your subconscious. If you find this hard to believe, remind yourself that many writers and musicians have come up with their greatest ideas in their dreams. For example, Robert Louis Stevenson dreamt the entire plots of *Treasure Island* and *Dr Jekyll and Mr Hyde*, while Beethoven and Mozart and, more recently, Keith Richards and Michael Jackson all first heard at least some of their musical compositions while they were asleep.

One final word: your speech is not set in stone. On the big day you must *listen* to previous speakers and then make sure you don't repeat anything already said. You must also be ready to briefly respond to any questions you may have been asked ('Do you remember that, John?'). And if some particular aspect of the day merits a special mention, then mention it ('I'm sure you'll all agree that the floral arrangements were magnificent').

So much for your preparation. Now let's consider your presentation.

PRESENTATION

Whatever cynics may tell you to the contrary, *what* you say is far more important than *how* you say it. Think about these TV personalities: Melvyn Bragg, David Bellamy, John McCririck, Gaby Roslin, Terry Wogan, Esther Rantzen, Sir David Frost, John Motson, Brian Walden, Anthea Turner, Barry Norman, Gordon Kennedy, Judi Spiers, Alan Titchmarsh, Ian McCaskill and Patrick Moore. I suggest they all have at least two things in common. First, they all communicate magnificently with their audiences because they come over as being genuinely interested in what they are talking about. Second, none of them is a particularly good speaker. Between them they share a multiplicity of speech defects, annoying personal mannerisms and difficult regional accents.

But, basically, who cares? After a few moments you adjust to any speech defect, mannerism or accent and you begin to concentrate on what really matters – the speaker's message. And who could fail to be impressed by the obvious enthusiasm and enjoyment which all these people convey? It is infectious – whether it is Melvyn Bragg passionately describing the legacy of the Pre-Raphaelite Brotherhood; David Bellamy breathlessly telling us all about the mating habits of the three-toed sloth; or John McCririck vehemently attacking all those nasty, greedy bookmakers.

It is no coincidence that ex-President Ronald Reagan was known as The Great Communicator even though he often forgot his lines and even the name of the person he was talking to. This didn't matter – in fact it may well have helped because he came over as the kind of man you could easily have had a chat with down at the pub, not as the leader of the most powerful nation in the world. In short, it showed he was human.

So the moral is clear: by far the most important thing is always *be yourself* and be totally sincere and enthusiastic in everything you say. Never fake sincerity – it won't fool anyone.

Once you have drafted a genuinely sincere speech – and only once you have – you can begin to work on your presentation. As Bob Monkhouse puts it: 'A speech is like a pair of shoes – it will always benefit from a little more polishing.'

There are three main ways to polish a speech – by rehearsing:

● in front of family or friends
● in front of a full-size mirror
● on videotape or audio cassette.

Have you ever listened to *Just a Minute!* on Radio 4? The idea of the programme is to be able to show you can talk on a given topic without:

● deviation
● hesitation, or
● repetition.

As you rehearse and review your performance ask yourself whether you have been guilty of any of these faults. Have you deviated from your central theme? Is everything you said strictly relevant? Have you hesitated unnecessarily? Pausing is fine, but drying up isn't. Your speech should flow naturally from point to point. Have you repeated yourself? It is all right to repeat the same words, but not the same quotations, jokes or anecdotes.

Then think about your body language. John McCririck's arm-waving histrionics are fine at a race course, but they would be disastrously out of place at a wedding reception. But, equally, you don't want to be so motionless that you look like a statue on loan from Madame Tussaud's. Try to relax, stand upright, and move easily and naturally as you speak.

Look at your presentation as others would. Be kind but critical. How could it be improved? Have you:

● Followed the KISS principle by using short words and short sentences in a short speech?

● Remembered that the day belongs to THE BRIDE?

● Made certain you are remaining focused on your central theme by responding to and/or proposing the toast?

● Ensured you are speaking slowly, clearly and naturally with a raised voice (but not shouting), pausing and varying your pace and pitch;

smiling, looking around the room and conversing with people – not
lecturing them?

● Eliminated any dull, negative, depressing, pompous, patronising,
embarrassing, offensive, overapologetic, overrevealing or inaccurate sections?

● Avoided any unnecessary words or lines; slang, jargon, in-jokes,
speech appendages (um, er, sort of, like, know what I mean?), or
awkward phrases?

● Corrected any pointless gestures, stiff expression or ugly or negative stance (crossed arms, hands in pockets)?

Rehearsal is very important, particularly to highlight any serious faults
that must be corrected, and to increase your confidence. However, it
should never be used to stifle your individuality or to try to change your
unique personality. Your audience will readily forgive any little gaffes
you make so long as you don't try to be someone you aren't and you
don't say things you obviously don't believe.

Tell yourself that you will give a great speech. And *believe* it. The
largely untapped power of positive thinking really is immense. Some
people may find this anonymous poem inspirational:

IF

If you think you are beaten, you are;
If you think you dare not, you don't;
If you'd like to win, but think you can't,
It's almost certain you won't;
If you think you'll lose, you've lost.
For out of the world we find
Success begins with a fellow's will –
It's all in the state of mind.
If you think you're outclassed, you are.
You've got to think high to rise;
You've got to be sure of yourself before
You can ever win a prize.
Life's battles don't always go
To the stronger or faster man,
But sooner or later the man who wins
Is the one who *thinks* he can.

2
Great Opening Lines

It is very important to have an opening line that really grabs your audience's attention. Entertainers call this having a hook. These are three of the best:

- the humour hook
- the quotation hook
- the anniversary hook.

The bride's father can begin his speech directly with one of these hooks, but the bridegroom and best man (and any other speakers) must remember to thank the previous speaker immediately before or soon after hooking their audience. However, to avoid boring repetition, I have included such thanks only with the first hook.

THE HUMOUR HOOK

Opening with a short and relevant joke or anecdote will help to relax you and get the audience laughing and even more on your side than they are already. Here are some possibilities:

Ladies and Gentlemen (thank you, Jim for those kind words . . .), as Henry VIII said to each of his wives in turn, 'I shall not keep you long'.

Ladies and Gentlemen – the ladies is over there [*pointing*], and the gents is over there [*pointing*].

Ladies and Gentlemen, I must admit that I have made a very similar speech to this before. Once to the Flat Earth Society, North-West Branch, once to the patients in Broadmoor, once to Aberdeen Naturalists' Group, and once to Penzance Haemorrhoid Sufferers

Society – a stand-up buffet. So to those of you who have heard this speech four times already, I apologise.

Ladies and Gentlemen, Clive just asked me, 'Would you like to speak now, or should we let our guests enjoy themselves a little longer?'

Ladies and Gentlemen, the last time I made a wedding speech someone at the rear shouted, 'I can't hear you!' – and a man sitting next to me yelled back, 'I'll change places with you!'

Ladies and Gentlemen, I can hardly wait to hear what I've got to say.

Ladies and Gentlemen, the last time I made a wedding speech a man fell asleep. I asked a pageboy to wake him, and do you know what the little horror replied? He said, 'You wake him. You were the one who put him to sleep.'

Ladies and Gentlemen, before I start speaking I have something to say.

Ladies and Gentlemen, I feel like the young Arab Sheik who inherited his father's harem. I know exactly what to do, but where on earth do I begin?

Ladies and Gentlemen – well Brian did ask me to begin with a gag.

Ladies and Gentlemen – who says flattery doesn't pay?

Ladies and Gentlemen, what can I say about Stephen that hasn't already been said in open court?

Ladies and Gentlemen, I'm only going to speak for a few moments because of my throat – if I go on too long, Ruth has threatened to cut it.

Ladies and Gentlemen, I've been asked to say a few words, so here goes . . . marzipan . . . chickens . . . pneumonia.

Ladies and Gentlemen, the management of the Queen Vic has requested that – in order to comply with local fire regulations – at the end of this speech, you all refrain from collapsing in the aisles throughout my twenty minute standing ovation.

Ladies and Gentlemen, since we must speak well of the dead, our only chance to knock them is while they're alive. So here goes . . .

Ladies and Gentlemen, my dad taught me always to remember the ABC and the XYZ of speechmaking. ABC: Always be concise. XYZ: Examine your zip [*look down*].

Ladies and Gentlemen, first the good news: when I saw Patrick's new suit/shirt/tie this morning I was absolutely speechless . . . Now the bad news: I've almost recovered from the shock, and the speech must go on.

Ladies and Gentlemen, I'd like to thank you all for coming . . . especially those of you who knew I'd be saying a few words but turned up anyway.

Ladies and Gentlemen, this is only the second time I've ever been a best man. I hope I did the job alright that time. The couple in question are at least still talking to me. Unfortunately, they're not actually talking to each other . . . but I'm sure that had absolutely nothing to do with me. Apparently Paula knew Piers had slept with her younger sister before I mentioned it in my speech. The fact that he slept with her mother came as a surprise. (Hugh Grant in *Four Weddings and a Funeral*). [If you use or adapt this opening, don't refer to a couple you really know!]

Ladies and Gentlemen, in the interests of political correctness and in order to spare our bridegroom's blushes, this speech will contain nothing controversial or embarrassing about John, but instead will refer only to the nice, pleasant side of his character . . . . Thank you and good afternoon [*make as if to sit down*].

Ladies and Gentlemen, that speech put me in mind of a steer's horns. There was a sharp point here and a solid point there . . . but there was an awful lot of bull in between.

Ladies and Gentlemen, you know I had a feeling it was going to be difficult to follow a speech by Don . . . and I was quite right . . . I couldn't follow a word of it.

[*After a formal introduction by a toastmaster*] Ladies and Gentlemen, did he say pray *for* the silence of John Smith?

[*After being called upon to give an impromptu speech*] Ladies and Gentlemen, I am totally unprepared for this, but, as Big Ben said to the Leaning Tower of Pisa, 'I've got the time if you've got the inclination'.

Ladies and gentlemen, my wife and I . . . (not a particularly funny hook but a very useful one for a bridegroom because it is guaranteed to raise howls of laughter, cheers and applause.)

THE QUOTATION HOOK

Here you simply begin your wedding speech with a short and relevant quotation. You will find plenty of these listed throughout the following chapter. It is far safer to use a serious quote rather than a cynical one. Begin with something like this:

Ladies and Gentlemen, 'Love is a great force in life, it is indeed the greatest of all things.' So said E.M. Forster, and E.M. knew what he was talking about . . .

Ladies and Gentlemen, it has been said that 'marriages are made in heaven'. Well, I can tell you, this marriage was made in my sitting room . . .

Sometimes a quotation associated with the bride's or bridegroom's occupation can be adapted to make an excellent and original opening. For example, here are a couple of adaptations suitable for members of the armed services:

Ladies and Gentlemen, 'Some talk of Alexander, and some of Hercules, of Hector and Lysander and such great names as these.' But I would rather talk about Captain and Mrs Mainwaring.

Ladies and Gentlemen, 'When he was a lad he served a term. As an office boy to an Attorney's firm. He cleaned the windows and he swept the floor. And he polished up the handle of the big front door. He polished up that handle so carefullee. That now he's the Ruler of the Queen's Navee' – well, almost, anyway.

THE ANNIVERSARY HOOK

Another wonderful way of grabbing an audience is to tell them that today is a truly historic day, not only because of the recent marriage but also because of other things that happened on this day in years gone by. It is best to mention two things as well as the marriage – probably a famous person's birth and some other memorable event.

As always, use your own words, but this is the sort of thing you should say:

Ladies and Gentlemen, this is a truly historic day! This day, the 18th of June, will always be remembered because of three earth-shattering events. Napoleon finally met his Waterloo at Waterloo in 1815, pop superstar Paul McCartney had his first day on earth in 1942, and on this day in 199-, Angus married Laura!

Ladies and Gentlemen, this is a day heavy with significance! This very day, the 1st of May, will always be associated with three of the most memorable events of the twentieth century. New York's Empire State Building opened in 1931, the Absolutely Fabulous Joanna Lumley was born in 1946, and on this day in 199-, Bernard married Lydia!

Get the idea? Below is a list of some famous blasts from the past. Simply look up the date of the wedding and you'll find an event and birth that also occurred on that day in years gone by. If they don't seem quite right for your speech, take a look at one or two of the specialist anniversary books listed on page 139.

FAMOUS ANNIVERSARIES

January

1 1964 First edition of *Top of the Pops* broadcast. 1967 Actress Michelle Holmes born.

2 1959 *Luna I*, world's first space probe, launched. 1967 Actress Nicolle Dickson born.

3 1924 British archaeologist Howard Carter discovered Tutankhamen's tomb. 1945 Rocker Stephen Stills born.

4 1960 REM's Michael Stipe born. 1961 *Billboard* published the world's first pop chart.

5   1931 Actor Robert Duvall born. 1933 Construction of California's Golden Gate Bridge began.

6   1838 Samuel Morse demonstrated his electric telegraph system for the first time. 1955 Funnyman Rowan Atkinson born.

7   1785 First balloon crossing of English Channel. 1948 Singer Kenny Loggins born.

8   1921 Chequers became official residence of British Prime Ministers. 1935 The King, Elvis Presley, born.

9   1799 Income Tax introduced in Britain as a so-called temporary measure. 1945 Led Zeppelin's Jimmy Page born.

10 1840 Penny Post introduced. 1945 Singer Rod Stewart born.

11 1864 Charing Cross railway station opened in London. 1963 Actor Jason Connery born.

12 1948 Actor Anthony Andrews born. 1970 First Jumbo jet transatlantic flight.

13 1923 The Independent Labour Party formed. 1961 Madness singer Graham 'Suggs' McPherson born.

14 1878 Queen Victoria made first private phone call in Britain. 1926 Alf Garnet (alias actor Warren Mitchell) born.

15 1559 Elizabeth I crowned. 1926 Rock legend Chuck Berry born.

16 1920 Prohibition era began in USA. 1960 Singer Sade born.

17 1956 Singer Paul Young born. 1983 Breakfast television began in Britain.

18 1778 Captain Cook discovered Hawaii. 1955 Actor Kevin Costner born.

19 1949 Singer Robert Palmer born. 1966 Indira Gandhi became India's first woman PM.

20 1841 Hong Kong ceded to Britain. 1947 Singer Malcolm McLaren born.

21 1925 The late and great Benny Hill born. 1976 Concorde made its first commercial flight.

22 1902 Marconi made his first radio transmission. 1940 Actor John Hurt born.

23 1899 Screen legend Humphrey Bogart born. 1985 House of Lords first televised.

24 1848 Californian Gold Rush began. 1951 Actor John Belushi born.

25 1327 Edward III became king. 1945 Actress Leigh Taylor-Young born.

26 1828 The Duke of Wellington became PM. 1925 Actor Paul Newman born.

27 1926 John Logie Baird gave his first public transmission of television. 1945 Pink Floyd's Nick Mason born.

28 1788 First Australian penal colony founded at Botany Bay. 1936 *M.A.S.H.*'s Hawkeye Pierce (alias actor Alan Alda) born.

29 1856 Victoria Cross instituted. 1945 Actor Tom Selleck born.

30 1649 Charles I lost his head. 1931 Actor Gene Hackman born.

31 1961 Singer Lloyd Cole born. 1969 The Beatles gave their final live performance – singing *Get Back* on the roof of the Apple building.

February

1 1901 Screen legend Clark Gable born. 1940 Captain Marvel first appeared in *Whiz Comics*.

2 1940 Del Boy (alias actor David Jason) born. 1989 The Soviet Union's nine-year military occupation of Afghanistan finally ended.

3 1947 Singer Melanie born. 1966 Russian *Luna 9* landed on the Moon.

4   1926 Malcolm Campbell broke the world land speed record. 1948 Rocker Alice Cooper born.

5   1952 TV astrologer Russell Grant born (Sun and Moon Aquarius, Libra Rising). 1989 Rupert Murdoch launched satellite Sky TV.

6   1950 Singer Natalie Cole born. 1952 Elizabeth II succeeded to the throne.

7   1959 UB40's Brian Travers born. 1964 Beatles arrived in the US and took the country by storm.

8   1931 Cult hero James Dean born. 1974 Skylab space station astronauts returned safely to earth after 85 days in space.

9   1942 Singer Carole King born. 1983 Derby winning racehorse Shergar disappeared.

10 1940 Singer Roberta Flack born. 1942 Glenn Miller presented with the first-ever gold disc – for *Chattanooga Choo Choo.*

11 1926 *Naked Gun* star Leslie Nielsen born. 1990 Nelson Mandela freed after 26 years' imprisonment.

12 1688 The 'Glorious Revolution' began. 1934 Actress Annette Crosbie born.

13 1692 Massacre of Glencoe. 1950 Singer Peter Gabriel born.

14 1929 The St Valentine's Day massacre in Chicago. 1946 Singer Gregory Hines born.

15 1959 UB40's Ali Campbell born. 1971 Decimalisation Day in Britain.

16 1946 *Dad's Army*'s Private Pike (alias actor Ian Lavender) born. 1959 Fidel Castro became Prime Minister of Cuba.

17 1863 International Red Cross founded in Geneva. 1934 Housewife megastar Dame Edna Everage born in Wagga-Wagga.

18 1930 Astronomer Clyde Tombaugh discovered the planet Pluto. 1960 Actress Greta Scacchi born.

19 1924 Screen bad guy Lee Marvin born. 1985 First episode of *Eastenders* broadcast.

20 1962 John Glenn became first US astronaut to orbit the earth. 1966 Supermodel Cindy Crawford born.

21 1947 TV cop Mary Beth Lacey (alias actress Tyne Daly) born. 1972 Nixon first US President to visit China.

22 1797 Last invasion of Britain (French at Fishguard). 1950 Actress-comedienne Julie Walters born.

23 1836 Siege of the Alamo began. 1955 Singer Howard Jones born.

24 1920 Nancy Astor became the first woman MP to speak in the House of Commons. 1940 Soccer legend Denis Law born.

25 1943 Guitarist George Harrison born. 1964 Muhammad Ali first became World Heavyweight Champion.

26 1815 Napoleon escaped from Elba. 1953 Singer Michael Bolton born.

27 1932 Actress Liz Taylor born. 1991 The Gulf War ended.

28 1900 Ladysmith relieved. 1942 Rolling Stone Brian Jones born.

29 1792 Gioacchino Rossini (you know, he wrote the *Lone Ranger* theme) born. 1956 Pakistan declared itself an Islamic Republic.

March

1 1555 Nostradamus's book of predictions published. 1958 Singer Nik Kershaw born.

2 1962 Singer Jon Bon Jovi born. 1969 Concorde made its maiden flight.

3 1958 Actress Miranda Richardson born. 1985 The miners' strike ended.

4   1890 Scotland's Forth Road Bridge opened. 1968 Actress Patsy Kensit born.

5   1946 Winston Churchill made his famous 'Iron Curtain' speech. 1952 Singer Elaine Paige born.

6   1836 The Alamo fell. 1936 *Bread*'s Ma Boswell (alias actress Jean Boht) born.

7   1876 Alexander Graham Bell patented his first telephone. 1952 Cricket legend Viv Richards born.

8   1917 Outbreak of Russian Revolution. 1958 Singer Gary Numan born.

9   1796 Napoleon married Josephine. 1958 Guitarist Robin Trower born.

10   1801 Britain's first national census carried out. 1964 Singer Neneh Cherry born.

11   1964 Funnyman Shane Richie born. 1985 Mikhail Gorbachev became leader of the USSR.

12   1946 Singer-actress Liza (with a Zee) Minelli born. 1969 Paul McCartney married Linda Eastman.

13   1781 William Herschel discovered the planet Uranus. 1960 U2's Adam Clayton born.

14   1917 The Russian February Revolution ended. 1933 Actor Michael Caine born (not a lot of people know that).

15   44 BC Julius Caesar assassinated. 1962 Singer Terence Trent D'Arby born.

16   1872 Wanderers became the first FA Cup winners. 1920 Horace Rumpole (alias actor Leo McKern) born.

17   1861 Italy became an independent kingdom. 1964 Actor Rob Lowe born.

18 1949 Snooker bad boy Alex Hurricane Higgins born. 1965 Cosmonaut Aleksey Leonov made the first space walk.

19 1932 Sydney Harbour Bridge opened. 1947 Actress Glenn Close born.

20 1957 Actor-director Spike Lee born. 1969 John Lennon married Yoko Ono.

21 1946 Actor Timothy Dalton born. 1963 Alcatraz prison closed.

22 1888 The English Football League founded. 1943 Singer George Benson born.

23 1848 First settlers landed in New Zealand. 1966 Pop star Marti Pellow born.

24 1603 James VI of Scotland became James I of England. 1971 Actor Keanu Reeves born.

25 1947 Superstar Elton John born. 1957 The Common Market established.

26 1944 Superstar Diana Ross born. 1973 Susan Shaw first woman to work in London's Stock Exchange in its 171-year history.

27 1942 Actor Michael York born. 1989 First democratic election for the Russian parliament took place.

28 1939 Spanish Civil War ended. 1976 Tennis ace Jennifer Capriati born.

29 1871 London's Royal Albert Hall opened. 1943 Funnyman Eric Idle born.

30 1867 USA bought Alaska from Russia. 1945 Guitar legend Eric Clapton born.

31 1889 The Eiffel Tower opened. 1943 Actor Christopher Walken born.

April
1 1918 RAF founded. 1962 TV personality and singer Philip Schofield born.

2 1960 Athlete Linford Christie born. 1982 Argentina foolishly invaded the Falklands.

3 1951 Madcap actor Eddie Murphy born. 1993 The Grand National declared void after two false starts.

4 1941 *Coronation Street*'s Jack Duckworth (alias actor Bill Tarmey) born. 1981 Bob Champion won the Grand National on Aldaniti.

5 1955 Radio personality Janice Long born. 1982 Royal Navy Task Force set sail for the Falklands.

6 1896 First modern Olympic Games opened in Athens. 1961 Impressionist Rory Bremner born.

7 1906 Mount Vesuvius erupted. 1939 TV presenter Sir David Frost born.

8 1963 Singer Julian Lennon born. 1986 Clint Eastwood elected mayor of Carmel.

9 1865 American Civil War ended. 1953 Actor Dennis Quaid born.

10 1961 TV and radio presenter Nicky Campbell born. 1989 Nick Faldo became first Briton to win golf's US Masters.

11 1929 Popeye made his first public appearance. 1966 Singer Lisa Stansfield born.

12 1948 TV joker Jeremy Beadle born. 1961 Yuri Gagarin became first man in space.

13 1936 Luton's Joe Payne scored a record ten goals in one game. 1946 Singer Al Green born.

14 1865 Abraham Lincoln assassinated. 1945 Rocker Richie Blackmore born.

15 1912 *Titanic* sank. 1959 Oscar-winning actress Emma Thompson born.

16 1918 Funnyman Spike Milligan born. 1995 27 million telephone numbers changed on British Telecom's Phoneday.

17 1946 TV host Henry Kelly born. 1956 Premium Bonds first issued.

18 1976 Actor Sean Maguire born. 1994 Cricketer Brian Lara completed his record-breaking Test innings of 375.

19 1936 Funnyman Dudley Moore born. 1958 Soccer legend Bobby Charlton scored the first of his record 49 goals for England.

20 1941 Actor Ryan O'Neal born. 1964 BBC2 first went on air.

21 753 BC Romulus founded Rome. 1926 Elizabeth II born.

22 1936 Arthur Daley (alias actor George Cole) born. 1972 John Fairfax and Sylvia Cook completed their marathon row across the Pacific.

23 1955 TV's Mike Smith born. 1968 First British decimal coins circulated.

24 1942 Superstar Barbra Streisand born. 1955 Patrick Moore's *Sky at Night* first televised.

25 1940 Actor Al Pacino born. 1982 British troops recaptured South Georgia from Argentina.

26 1960 Duran Duran's Roger Taylor born. 1994 First free elections held in South Africa.

27 1969 Singer Mica Paris born. 1995 Snooker's Stephen Hendry scored a maximum 147 on his way to successfully defending his World Championship.

28 1770 Captain Cook landed at Botany Bay. 1937 Actor Jack Nicholson born.

29 1958 Actress Michelle Pfeiffer born. 1986 Halley's comet made its last visit here until the year 2062.

30 1946 Actor Leslie Grantham born. 1975 The Vietnam War ended.

May

1 1931 New York's Empire State Building opened. 1946 The Absolutely Fabulous Joanna Lumley born.

2 1945 Steppenwolf's Goldy McJohn born. 1963 Beatles had their first UK number one hit.

3 1492 Columbus arrived in Jamaica instead of China as he'd hoped. 1960 Funnyman Ben Elton born.

4 1780 First Derby run. 1952 Entertainer Michael Barrymore born.

5 1943 TV globe-trotter Michael Palin born. 1980 The SAS stormed the Iranian Embassy in London.

6 1953 Soccer's Graeme Souness born. 1994 The Channel Tunnel officially opened.

7 1756 Nelson's ship HMS *Victory* launched. 1939 Singer Jimmy Ruffin born.

8 1954 Entertainer Gary Wilmot born. 1995 Britain celebrated the 50th anniversary of victory over Hitler's Germany.

9 1671 Thomas Blood stole the Crown Jewels. 1949 Singer Billy Joel born.

10 1857 Outbreak of Indian Mutiny. 1960 U2's Bono born.

11 1962 Actress Natasha Richardson born. 1981 Sir Andrew Lloyd Webber's musical *Cats* opened in London.

12 1937 Coronation of George VI. 1942 *Eastenders'* Pam St Clement born.

13 1607 Jamestown, the first English settlement in America, established. 1950 Pop legend Stevie Wonder born.

14 1796 Physician Edward Jenner used the world's first vaccine. 1926 The late and great Eric Morecambe born.

15 1953 Musician Mike Oldfield born. 1988 Russia began pulling out of Afghanistan after an eight-year occupation.

16   1929 First Oscars awarded. 1966 Singer Janet Jackson born.

17   1956 Boxing legend Sugar Ray Leonard born. 1993 Rebecca Stephens first British woman to conquer Everest.

18   1804 Napoleon proclaimed Emperor of France. 1958 Singer Toyah Wilcox born.

19   1953 Comedienne Victoria Wood born. 1991 Helen Sharman became the first Briton in space.

20   1588 The ill-fated Spanish Armada set sail from Lisbon. 1946 Singer-actress Cher born.

21   1948 Singer Leo Sayer born. 1979 Elton John became the first western rock star to perform in Russia.

22   1908 The Wright brothers patented the world's first aeroplane. 1959 Singer Morrissey born.

23   1498 Vasco da Gama became the first European to reach India by sea. 1936 Actress Joan Collins born.

24   1844 Samuel Morse sent world's first telegraph message. 1941 Singer-songwriter Bob Dylan born.

25   1935 Athlete Jesse Owens set an amazing six world records in 45 minutes. 1958 Singer Paul Weller born.

26   1865 The American Civil War ended. 1948 Singer Stevie Nicks born.

27   1941 The *Bismarck* was sunk by the British navy. 1943 Our Cilla born.

28   1945 Singer-guitarist John Fogerty born. 1967 Sir Francis Chichester completed his round-the-world journey in *Gipsy Moth IV*.

29   1949 Status Quo's Francis Rossi born. 1953 Hillary and Tenzing conquered Everest.

30 1959 First public hovercraft demonstration. 1963 *Coronation Street*'s Sally Webster (alias actress Sally Whittaker) born.

31 1961 Comedian Harry Enfield born. 1965 Jim Clark became the first British driver to win the Indianapolis 500.

June

1   1926 Screen legend Marilyn Monroe born. 1967 The Beatles released the classic *Sergeant Pepper's Lonely Hearts' Club Band*.

2   1941 Rolling Stones' drummer Charlie Watts born. 1953 Coronation of Elizabeth II.

3   1950 Rocker Suzi Quatro born. 1981 Shergar won the Derby by a record 10 lengths.

4   1913 Suffragette Emily Davison threw herself under the King's horse in the Derby. 1930 *Eastenders*' Arthur Fowler (alias Bill Treacher) born.

5   1941 Singer-songwriter Harry Nilsson born. 1975 Suez Canal reopened after eight years' closure.

6   1947 Freddy Krueger star Robert Englund born. 1994 Cricketer Brian Lara completed his record-breaking innings of 501 n.o.

7   1962 Prefab Sprout's Paddy McAloon born. 1982 Elvis Presley's mansion Graceland opened to the public for the first time.

8   1960 Simply Red's Mick Hucknall born. 1978 Dame Naomi James completed her epic solo circumnavigation of the world.

9   1934 Donald Duck made his film debut. 1961 Actor Michael J. Fox born.

10 1942 *The Krypton Factor*'s Gordon Burns born. 1986 Bob Geldof given an honorary knighthood for his efforts to relieve world famine.

11 1935 Actor Gene Wilder born. 1975 First oil pumped ashore from the North Sea.

12 1945 Soccer legend Pat Jennings born. 1979 Bryan Allen crossed the Channel in a pedal boat.

13 1900 Boxer Rising in China. 1955 Soccer's Alan Hansen born.

14 1969 Tennis ace Steffi Graf born. 1982 Union Jack hoisted in Port Stanley after surrender of Argentinian troops.

15 1215 Magna Carta signed, sealed and delivered. 1950 Slade singer Noddy Holder born.

16 1946 Actor Simon Williams born. 1963 Valentina Tereshkova became the first woman in space.

17 1775 Britain defeated America at the Battle of Bunker Hill. 1946 Singer-songwriter Barry Manilow born.

18 1815 Napoleon met his Waterloo at Waterloo. 1942 Superstar Paul McCartney born.

19 1829 Sir Robert Peel founded the Metropolitan Police. 1954 Actress Kathleen Turner born.

20 1837 Victoria became Queen. 1966 Actress Nicole Kidman born.

21 1944 The Kinks' Ray Davies born. 1970 Brazil won soccer's World Cup for the third time and so kept the trophy permanently.

22 1937 Joe Louis began his 11-year reign as world heavyweight boxing champion. 1949 Actress Meryl Streep born.

23 1911 Coronation of George V. 1955 TV's Maggie Philbin born.

24 1877 St John Ambulance Brigade founded. 1944 Rock legend Jeff Beck born.

25 1876 Battle of the Little Bighorn (Custer's Last Stand). 1963 Singer George Michael born.

26 1857 First Victoria Cross awarded. 1956 Singer Chris Isaak born.

27 1962 Singer Michael Ball born. 1988 Dave Hurst and Alan Matthews became first blind mountaineers to scale Mont Blanc.

28 1926 Madcap actor-director Mel Brooks born. 1948 Berlin Airlift began.

29 1944 Actor Gary Busey born. 1986 Richard Branson's boat *Virgin Atlantic Challenger II* completed fastest Atlantic crossing.

30 1859 Charles Blondin crossed the Niagara Falls on a tightrope. 1961 TV host Nino Firetto born.

July

1   1838 Charles Darwin first announced his theory of evolution. 1952 Funnyman Dan Aykroyd born.

2   1865 William Booth founded the Salvation Army. 1956 Actress Jerry Hall born.

3   1962 Actor Tom Cruise born. 1987 Richard Branson completed his transatlantic hot-air balloon crossing.

4   1776 American Declaration of Independence approved by Congress. 1938 Singer Bill Withers born.

5   1950 Singer Huey Lewis born. 1980 Bjorn Borg won his fifth successive Wimbledon singles title.

6   1685 Last battle on English soil (Sedgemoor, Somerset). 1946 John J. Rambo (alias actor Sylvester Stallone) born.

7   1940 Drummer Ringo Starr born. 1988 Live Aid concerts in London and Philadelphia raised millions for famine relief.

8   1951 Actress Anjelica Huston born. 1978 Reinhold Messner and Peter Habeler first mountaineers to climb Everest without the use of oxygen.

9   1947 Betrothal of the future Queen Elizabeth II to Philip announced. 1956 Actor Tom Hanks born.

10 1900 The Paris Metro opened. 1962 *Big Breakfast*'s Gaby Roslin born.

11 1950 Andy Pandy made his TV debut. 1959 Singer Suzanne Vega born.

12 1958 The Absolutely Fabulous Jennifer Saunders born. 1982 The Falklands War officially ended.

13 1942 Actor Harrison Ford born. 1985 Live Aid pop concerts for African famine victims.

14 1789 The Bastille stormed. 1950 Fashion designer Bruce Oldfield born.

15 1881 Sheriff Pat Garrett shot Billy the Kid. 1946 Singer Linda Ronstadt born.

16 1790 Washington DC became capital of USA. 1907 Screen legend Barbara Stanwyck born.

17 1917 The British Royal Family changed its name to Windsor. 1952 Actor David Hasselhoff born.

18 1941 Singer Martha Reeves born. 1955 Disneyland opened in California.

19 1545 Henry VIII's battleship the *Mary Rose* sank in the Solent. 1969 Singer Gabrielle born.

20 1837 London's Euston Station opened. 1946 *Eastenders'* Pauline Fowler (alias actress Wendy Richard) born.

21 1952 Funnyman Robin Williams born. 1969 Astronaut Neil Armstrong took a giant step for mankind.

22 1844 Rev. William Spooner, originator of spoonerisms, porn in Breston. 1934 US baddie John Dillinger tried to rob one bank too many.

23 1759 Construction of Nelson's flagship, HMS *Victory* began. 1947 Singer-actor David Essex born.

24 1936 The Speaking Clock spoke for the first time. 1951 Wonder Woman Lynda Carter born.

25   1909 Louis Bleriot made first cross-Channel flight. 1978 Britain's first test tube baby, Louise Joy Brown, born.

26   1908 The USA's FBI founded in Washington. 1943 Rolling Stone Mick Jagger born.

27   1937 Actor Bill Cosby born. 1953 Korean War ended.

28   1936 Cricket legend Sir Garfield Sobers born. 1986 Laura Davies first Englishwoman to win golf's US Women's Open.

29   1558 The English fleet defeated the Spanish Armada. 1966 Champion hurdler Sally Gunnell born.

30   1947 Iron-pumping Arnold Schwarzenegger born. 1966 England won soccer's World Cup.

31   1944 Actress Geraldine Chaplin born. 1956 Cricketer Jim Laker completed his record-breaking 19 for 90 haul against the Aussies.

August

1   1798 Nelson won the Battle of the Nile. 1932 *Emmerdale*'s Frank Tate (alias actor Norman Bowler) born.

2   1876 Wild Bill Hickok shot by Jack McCall in Deadwood. 1932 Actor Peter O'Toole born.

3   1778 La Scala Opera House opened in Milan. 1940 Actor Martin Sheen born.

4   1914 Outbreak of World War I. 1943 Actress Georgina Hale born.

5   1901 Britain's first cinema opened. 1906 Supersleuth Miss Jane Marple (alias actress Joan Hickson) born.

6   1947 Actor Oliver Tobias born. 1971 Chay Blyth completed his epic non-stop circumnavigation of the world.

7   1711 First Royal Ascot Race Meeting held. 1961 Funnyman Brian Conley born.

8   1961 U2 guitarist The Edge born. 1963 The Great Train Robbery took place.

9   1961 Singer Whitney Houston born. 1979 Nude sunbathing became legal on Cliff Beach, Brighton.

10 1675 Royal Observatory at Greenwich opened. 1947 Jethro Tull's Ian Anderson born.

11 1942 London's New Waterloo Bridge opened. 1954 Singer Joe Jackson born.

12 1908 First Model T Ford car produced. 1949 Dire Straits' Mark Knopfler born.

13 1704 Duke of Marlborough won Battle of Blenheim. 1952 Model Marie Helvin born.

14 1945 Japan surrendered unconditionally thereby ending World War II. 1961 Singer Sarah Brightman born.

15 1947 Actress Jenny Hanley born. 1969 The first Woodstock rock festival opened in upstate New York.

16 1958 Madonna (the outrageous singer, not the outrageous footballer) born. 1975 Phil Collins became Genesis's lead singer.

17 1896 Canadian Klondike Goldrush began. 1943 Actor Robert De Niro born.

18 1937 Actor Robert Redford born. 1948 12-year-old Lester Piggott rode his first winner.

19 1648 The Parliamentarians defeated the Royalists at Preston during the English Civil War. 1945 Rocker Ian Gillan born.

20 1947 Singer Robert Plant born. 1980 Reinhold Messner first to climb Everest solo.

21 1933 Film buff Barry Norman born – and why not? 1988 Pubs first allowed to stay open 12 hours a day.

22   1642 The English Civil War began. 1961 Tears For Fears' Roland Orzabel born.

23   1939 British driver John Cobb broke the world land speed record. 1962 Happy Mondays' singer Shaun Ryder born.

24   79AD Pompeii destroyed by the eruption of Vesuvius. 1958 Actor Steve Guttenberg born.

25   1875 Captain Matthew Webb first to swim the English Channel. 1953 Singer-songwriter Elvis Costello born.

26   55 BC Julius Caesar came, saw and conquered. 1980 Actor Macaulay Culkin born.

27   1883 Krakatoa erupted. 1961 TV presenter Mark Curry born.

28   1961 Singer Kim Appleby born. 1963 Dr Martin Luther King delivered his famous 'I have a dream' speech in Washington.

29   1958 Superstar Michael Jackson born. 1966 The Beatles played their final live concert – at Candlestick Park, San Francisco.

30   1860 Britain's first tramcar took to the streets – in Birkenhead. 1955 Swing Out Sister's Martin Jackson born.

31   1949 Actor Richard Gere born. 1968 Gary Sobers smashed six sixes in an over for Nottinghamshire.

September
1   1957 Singer Gloria Estefan born. 1972 Bobby Fisher became world chess champion.

2   1666 The Great Fire of London broke out. 1966 Soccer's Steve Staunton born.

3   1939 Britain declared war on Hitler's Germany. 1940 Liverpool housewife Shirley Valentine (alias actress Pauline Collins) born.

4   1961 *Coronation Street*'s Curly Watts (alias actor Kevin Kennedy) born. 1964 Forth Road Bridge opened.

5   1885 Arbroath hammered Bon Accord by a record 36–0. 1935 *Coronation Street*'s Mike Baldwin (alias actor Johnny Briggs) born.

6   1620 The *Mayflower* set sail for the New World. 1961 A-ha's Pal Waaktaar born.

7   1951 Rocker Chrissie Hynde born. 1986 Bishop Desmond Tutu enthroned as Archbishop of Cape Town.

8   1664 English captured New Amsterdam and renamed it New York. 1946 Rock legend Freddie Mercury born.

9   1952 Rock star Dave Stewart born. 1978 Eighteen-year-old Czech tennis star Martina Navratilova asked for political asylum in America.

10 1944 The Who's John Entwistle born. 1967 Gibraltar voted overwhelmingly to remain British.

11 1940 Film director Brian De Palma born. 1978 BBC broadcast first episode of *Dallas*.

12 1878 Cleopatra's Needle erected on the Thames Embankment. 1944 Singer Barry White born.

13 1957 *The Mousetrap* became Britain's longest-running West End play. 1959 Impressionist Bobby Davro born.

14 1752 Britain adopted the Gregorian calendar. 1939 *Coronation Street*'s Alma Baldwin (alias actress Amanda Barrie) born.

15 1940 Britain won the Battle of Britain. 1946 Film director Oliver Stone born.

16 1927 Lieutenant Columbo (alias actor Peter Falk) born. 1968 The Post Office introduced its two-tier delivery service.

17 1931 Long-playing records invented. 1950 *Coronation Street*'s Maureen Holdsworth (alias actress Sherrie Hewson) born.

18 1789 Blackpool illuminations switched on for the first time. 1958 TV personality Linda Lusardi born.

19   1949 Actress Twiggy Lawson born. 1975 First episode of *Fawlty Towers* televised.

20   1934 Actress Sophia Loren born. 1967 The *QEII* launched.

21   1930 *Dallas*'s J.R. Ewing (alias actor Larry Hagman) born. 1965 BP struck oil in North Sea.

22   1955 Commercial television began in Britain. 1971 Singer Chesney Hawkes born.

23   1949 The Boss, Bruce Springsteen, born in the USA. 1974 The BBC's Ceefax teletext service began.

24   1941 Vegetarian cookery expert Linda McCartney born. 1975 Dougal Haston and Doug Scott scaled south-west face of Everest.

25   1066 Battle of Stamford Bridge (no, Chelsea weren't playing). 1944 Actor Michael Douglas born.

26   1934 The *Queen Mary* launched. 1962 Everything But The Girl singer Tracy Thorn born.

27   1825 Stockton to Darlington rail line opened. 1947 Rock singer Meatloaf born.

28   1745 The National Anthem first sung in public. 1952 Actress Sylvia Kristel born.

29   1970 Actress Emily Lloyd born. 1983 Lady Mary Donaldson elected first woman Lord Mayor of London.

30   1931 Actress Angie Dickenson born. 1967 Radio 1 first went on air.

October

1   1920 Actor Walter Matthau born. 1971 Disney World opened in Florida.

2   1950 Charlie Brown and Snoopy made their first public apperance. 1951 Singer Sting born.

3   1899 Boer War began. 1941 Pop twister Chubby Checker born.

4   1957 *Sputnik*, first satellite to orbit earth, launched. 1959 Pet Shop Boy Chris Lowe born.

5   1936 The Jarrow March began. 1954 Rocker Sir Bob Geldof born.

6   1930 *Coronation Street*'s Emily Bishop (alias actress Eileen Derbyshire) born. 1985 Nigel Mansell won his first Grand Prix.

7   1769 Captain Cook landed in New Zealand. 1939 TV personality Clive James born.

8   1949 *Aliens* star Sigourney Weaver born. 1965 London's Post Office Tower opened.

9   1888 The Washington Monument unveiled. 1940 Pop legend John Lennon born.

10 1946 Actor Charles Dance born. 1972 Sir John Betjeman appointed Poet Laureate.

11 1957 Comedienne Dawn French born. 1982 Henry VIII's warship *Mary Rose* raised from Portsmouth Harbour.

12 1954 Entertainer Les Dennis born. 1986 The Queen was first British monarch to visit China.

13 1941 Singer-songwriter Paul Simon born. 1982 Scott Weiland completed the Detroit marathon in 4 hours 8 minutes – running backwards.

14 1066 Battle of Hastings. 1940 Peter Pan pop singer Cliff Richard born.

15 1948 Singer Chris de Burgh born. 1962 Amnesty International founded in London.

16 1815 Napoleon exiled to St Helena. 1925 Cabot Cove's Jessica Fletcher (alias actress Angela Lansbury) born.

17   1931 Al Capone sentenced to 11 years' imprisonment for income tax evasion. 1948 Actress Margot Kidder born.

18   1887 The USA bought Alaska from Russia. 1927 Actor George C. Scott born.

19   1812 Napoleon began his retreat from Moscow. 1963 Singer Sinitta born.

20   1946 Muffin the Mule made his TV debut. 1958 Level 42's Mark King born.

21   1805 Battle of Trafalgar. 1957 Pop's Julian Cope born.

22   1797 André-Jacques Garnerin made the first-ever parachute jump. 1952 Actor Jeff Goldblum born.

23   1642 Battle of Edge Hill. 1940 Soccer legend Pelé born.

24   1936 Ex-Rolling Stone Bill Wyman born. 1945 The United Nations came into existence.

25   1415 Henry V defeated the French at Agincourt. 1942 Singer Helen Reddy born.

26   1881 Gunfight at the OK Corral. 1957 Actress Julie Dawn Cole born.

27   1939 Torquay hotelier Basil Fawlty (alias actor John Cleese) born. 1958 *Blue Peter* first televised.

28   1886 Statue of Liberty unveiled. 1967 *Pretty Woman* star Julia Roberts born.

29   1929 Wall Street Crash. 1947 Actor Richard Dreyfuss born.

30   1938 People thought Martians had landed when Orson Welles read *The War of the Worlds* on US radio. 1943 Singer Grace Slick born.

31   1951 Zebra crossings introduced in Britain. 1961 U2's Larry Mullen born.

November

1   1512 Michelangelo unveiled the ceiling of the Sistine Chapel. 1963 Def Leppard's Rick Allen born.

2   1961 Singer k. d. lang born. 1964 First episode of *Crossroads* broadcast.

3   1921 *Death Wish* star Charles Bronson born. 1957 Laika became the first dog in space.

4   1605 Guy Fawkes arrested for attempting to blow up Parliament – yes, it *was* on the 4th November. 1954 Squeeze singer Chris Difford born.

5   1909 Britain's first Woolworth store opened – in Liverpool. 1959 Singer Bryan Adams born.

6   1860 Abraham Lincoln elected President of USA. 1926 Comedian Frank Carson born.

7   1917 The October Revolution (yes October) began in Russia. 1943 Singer-songwriter Joni Mitchell born.

8   1939 *Coronation Street's* Vera Duckworth (alias actress Elizabeth Dawn) born. 1974 Lord Lucan disappeared.

9   1951 *Incredible Hulk* star Lou Ferrigno born. 1960 John F. Kennedy elected US president.

10 1940 Monster Raving Loony Party leader Screaming Lord Sutch born. 1989 The hated Berlin Wall dismantled.

11 1918 World War I ended. 1956 Heaven 17's Glenn Gregory born.

12 1927 First veteran car rally from London to Brighton. 1945 Singer Neil Young born.

13 1914 Mrs Mary Phelps Jacob patented her new uplifting invention – the bra. 1949 Actress Whoopi Goldberg born.

14 1953 Singer Alexander O'Neal born. 1994 First public train service ran – or rather crawled – through the Channel Tunnel.

15   1952 Derrick Evans, better known as GMTV's Mr Motivator, born. 1969 Britain's first colour TV advertisement screened, mainly in green – it was for Birds Eye Peas.

16   1532 Spanish adventurer Pizarro conquered the Incas. 1961 Boxer Frank Bruno born (Know what I mean, 'Arry?).

17   1869 The Suez Canal opened. 1944 Actor Danny DeVito born.

18   1928 Mickey Mouse made his film debut. 1960 Singer Kim Wilde born.

19   1963 Actress Meg Ryan born. 1994 First-ever National Lottery draw made.

20   1947 Princess Elizabeth married Lieutenant Philip Mountbatten. 1959 Actress Bo Derek born.

21   1620 The *Mayflower* arrived in the New World. 1945 Actress Goldie Hawn born.

22   1946 The world's first ballpoint pens went on sale. 1958 Actress Jamie Lee Curtis born.

23   1943 *Coronation Street*'s Audrey Roberts (alias actress Sue Nicholls) born. 1963 *Dr Who*'s Tardis materialised for the first time.

24   1942 Funnyman Billy Connolly born. 1952 Agatha Christie's play *The Mousetrap* opened at the Ambassadors, London.

25   1944 ELO's drummer Bev Bevan born. 1953 England put three goals past Hungary at Wembley – but let in six.

26   1938 Simply the Best singer Tina Turner born. 1968 Supergroup Cream played their final concert at London's Albert Hall.

27   1582 Shakespeare married Anne Hathaway. 1942 Pop legend Jimi Hendrix born.

28   1944 Singer-songwriter Randy Newman born. 1990 Maggie Thatcher resigned.

29 1962 Britain and France agreed to build Concorde. 1973 Soccer's Ryan Giggs dribbled for the first time.

30 1580 Sir Francis Drake completed his circumnavigation of the world in the *Golden Hind*. 1945 Deep Purple's Roger Glover born.

December

1 1940 Actor Richard Pryor born. 1990 Britain was joined to continental Europe as the two Channel Tunnel construction teams met in the middle.

2 1697 Sir Christopher Wren's new St Paul's Cathedral opened. 1960 Def Leppard's Rick Savage born.

3 1948 Rocker Ozzie Osbourne born. 1967 Dr Christian Barnard performed the world's first heart transplant operation.

4 1154 Nicholas Breakspear became the first and only English Pope – Adrian IV. 1949 Actor Jeff Bridges born.

5 1872 The *Marie Celeste* found adrift and unmanned near the Azores. 1935 Rock legend Little Richard born.

6 1877 Thomas Edison made the first sound recording. 1944 TV presenter Jonathan King born.

7 1941 Japan attacked the US fleet in Pearl Harbor. 1949 Singer Tom Waits born.

8 1863 Britain's Tom King (the boxer, not the politician) became first world heavyweight champion. 1953 Actress Kim Basinger born.

9 1950 Singer Joan Armatrading born. 1960 First episode of *Coronation Street* broadcast.

10 1901 First Nobel Prizes awarded. 1952 *L.A. Law*'s Grace Van Owen (alias actress Susan Dey) born.

11 1936 King Edward VIII gave up the crown so he could marry Wallis Simpson. 1954 Singer Jermaine Jackson born.

12 1901 Marconi made first transatlantic wireless transmission. 1915 Ol' Blue Eyes, Frank Sinatra, born.

13 1577 Sir Francis Drake began his circumnavigation of the world in the *Golden Hind*. 1953 Entertainer Jim Davidson born.

14 1911 Roald Amundsen first man to reach the South Pole. 1954 *'Allo 'Allo* star Vicki Michelle born.

15 1916 The nine-month Battle of Verdun finally ended. 1964 *Coronation Street*'s Kevin Webster (alias actor Michael Le Vell) born.

16 1773 The Boston Tea Party. 1949 ZZ Top's Billy Gibbons born.

17 1903 Orville Wright made first ever aeroplane flight. 1945 Actor Christopher Cazenove born.

18 1865 Slavery abolished in USA. 1947 Film director Steven Spielberg born.

19 1963 *Flashdance* star Jennifer Beals born. 1984 Britain and China signed the agreement which will return Hong Kong to China in 1997.

20 1803 The biggest land deal in history – The Louisiana Purchase – doubled the size of the USA at the stroke of a quill. 1946 Fork-bending Uri Geller born.

21 1913 The world's first crossword puzzle published. 1940 Rock legend Frank Zappa born.

22 1895 Wilhelm Röntgen discovered X-rays. 1946 Noel Edmonds' Crinkley Bottom seen for the first time.

23 1888 Vincent Van Gogh cut off part of his left ear. 1955 Iron Maiden's Dave Murray born.

24 1945 Motorhead's Lemmy born. 1968 *Apollo 8* first manned spaceship to orbit the moon.

25 1066 William the Conquerer crowned at Westminster Abbey. 1949 Actress Sissy Spacek born.

26 1898 The Curies discovered radium. 1927 Actor Denis Quilley born.

27 1831 Darwin set sail for the Galapagos Islands in HMS *Beagle*. 1974 Singer Vanessa Paradis born.

28 1926 Victoria completed their record-breaking innings of 1107 runs against New South Wales. 1954 Actor Denzel Washington born.

29 1930 Radio Luxembourg first went on air. 1947 Actor Ted Danson born.

30 1916 Russian mystic Rasputin was poisoned, shot and finally drowned. 1964 Actress Sophie Ward born.

31 1923 The chimes of Big Ben first heard by radio listeners. 1948 Singer Donna Summer born.

How to Plan a Wedding
Mary Kilborn

Expertly written by a counsellor with the Scottish Marriage Guidance Council, this popular book fills the need for a practical guide on the questions every couple or their parents need to consider. With lots of helpful headings, and quick checklists, the book covers getting engaged, buying the ring, making announcements, wedding ceremonies and marriage vows, organising the reception, speeches, gifts, honeymoon arrangements and more. Now in its third edition, the book also contains helpful advice on such things as mixed marriages, the pregnant bride, how to cope with divorced parents, and even how to get married on a beach in the Bahamas. With specimen invitation cards, weddings lists, useful contacts, and more. 'Recommended reading.' *Northern Echo*.

£7.99, 128 pp illus. 1 85703 154 7. 3rd edition.

Please add postage & packing (UK £1 per copy, Europe £2 per copy, World £3 per copy airmail).

How To Books Ltd, Plymbridge House, Estover Road, Plymouth PL6 7PZ, United Kingdom. Tel: (01752) 695745. Fax: (01752) 695699. Telex: 45635.

Credit card orders may be faxed or phoned.

3
Useful Quotations

An apt quotation about love or marriage can really lift a wedding speech. But don't overdo it; quoting people can sound pompous. Just give one or two appropriate lines and do it in a very casual way. If you are quoting somebody famous, make it clear that you had to look it up – the last thing you want is to sound like a *Mastermind* contestant specialising in Quotations. Say something like:

> I am reminded of the words of Groucho Marx – reminded I should say by my wife, who looked it up last night . . .

Alternatively, you could make it clear that you are reading a short extract from a book:

> I would like to read you the first two lines of one of Linda's favourite poems . . .

If you want to quote someone less well known, don't mention him or her by name. If you do, the reaction will probably be: 'Who?' Rather, say something like:

> Someone once said that . . ., or, It has been said that . . .

Unfortunately many of the best quotes about love and marriage are quite cynical, and there is absolutely no place for anything negative or sneering in a wedding speech. A very simple way to get round this is to make it very clear that any cynical quote you use most certainly does *not* apply to the happy couple:

> Someone once said that he had gone into marriage with his eyes closed – her father had closed one of them and her brother had closed the other. Well, all I can say is that William went into his

50

marriage with his eyes wide open. And seeing how beautiful Mary looks today, who could blame him?

There are thousands of good quotations about love and marriage. *The Oxford Dictionary of Quotations* alone has well over five hundred of them. I have listed some of the best below. You'll find something old, something new, something borrowed, but definitely nothing blue. However, if you can't find anything suitable, look through one or more of the books listed under 'Further Reading' at the back of this book. Alternatively, you could quote something you have heard or read that seems particularly appropriate for the occasion. If you quote a line or two from a song, make sure that it is specific enough to mean something to the bride and bridegroom, yet is still general enough to be appreciated by the rest of the audience. I recently heard a bridegroom say this, and it almost brought the house down:

Well, Liz, in the words of your favourite Carpenters' song, 'We've only just begun. So much of life ahead. A kiss for luck [*he blew her a kiss*] and we're on our way.' Yes, Liz, we've only just begun!

Later they played the record and there wasn't a dry eye in the house.

For the less adventurous speaker, here is a sample of more conventional quotations.

LOVE AND MARRIAGE

There is no more lovely, friendly and charming relationship, communion or company than a good marriage (Martin Luther).

Love is the light and sunshine of life. We cannot fully enjoy ourselves, or anything else, unless someone we love enjoys it with us (Sir John Avebury).

Love is the wine of existence (Henry Ward Beecher).

The great secret of successful marriage is to treat all disasters as incidents and none of the incidents as disasters (Harold Nicolson).

Love is a great force in life; it is indeed the greatest of all things (E.M. Forster).

Eternal love, and everlasting love (Thomas Otway).

Love is more than gold or great riches (John Lydgate).

Love is the only weapon we need (Rev H.R.L. Sheppard).

When one loves somebody everything is clear – where to go, what to do – it all takes care of itself and one doesn't have to ask anybody about anything (Maxim Gorky).

Of all forms of caution, caution in love is perhaps the most fatal to true happiness (Bertrand Russell).

To fear love is to fear life, and those who fear life are already three parts dead (Bertrand Russell).

Success in marriage is more than *finding* the right person; it is *being* the right person (Rabbi B.R. Bricker).

Marriage is a mutual partnership if both parties know when to be mute (Anon).

I love you more than yesterday and less than tomorrow (Edmond Rostand).

A toast to sweethearts. May all sweethearts become married couples and may all married couples remain sweethearts (Anon).

Marriage halves our griefs, doubles our joys, and quadruples our expenses (Vincent Lean).

The love we give away is the only love we keep (Elbert Hubbard).

The trouble was, I went into marriage with both eyes closed – her father closed one and her brother closed the other (Max Kauffman).

Love doesn't make the world go round. Love is what makes the ride worthwhile (Franklin P. Jones).

A successful marriage is an edifice that must be rebuilt every day (André Maurois).

A marriage is a long conversation which always seems too short (André Maurois).

Marriage is an investment that pays dividends if you pay interest (Bob Monkhouse).

A successful marriage involves falling in love many times – with the same person (Bob Monkhouse).

Husbands are like fires . . . they go out when unattended (Zsa Zsa Gabor).

Marriage is a great institution – no family should be without it (Bob Hope).

Love is like oxygen. You get too much you get so high — not enough you're going to die (D. Ream's Peter Cunnah).

You can always tell when a husband is lying – his lips move (Ken Livingston MP).

How absurd and delicious it is to fall in love with somebody younger than yourself (Barbara Pym).

The critical period in matrimony is breakfast time (A.P. Herbert).

Never go to bed mad. Stay up and fight (Phyllis Diller).

When a man brings his wife flowers for no reason – there's a reason (Molly McGee).

Love makes the world go around (Proverb).

Whenever you're wrong, admit it; whenever you're right, shut up (Ogden Nash).

The reason husbands and wives do not understand each other is because they belong to different sexes (Dorothy Dix).

True love never grows old (Proverb).

Like fingerprints, all marriages are different (George Bernard Shaw).

Marriage is so popular because it combines the maximum of temptation with the maximum of opportunity (George Bernard Shaw).

Love does not consist of gazing at each other but in looking outward together in the same direction (Antoine de Saint-Exupéry).

Marriage is like holding an electric wire – it can be shocking but you can't let go (Anon).

Their love makes Vesuvius look like a damp sparkler (Alida Baxter).

Don't marry anyone until you've seen them drunk (Anon).

Where love is concerned, too much is not enough (Anon).

Any man who says he can see through a woman is missing a lot (Groucho Marx).

All unhappy marriages come from the husband having brains (P.G. Woodhouse).

Marriage is like pleading guilty with an indefinite sentence and no parole (Horace Rumpole, with a little help from John Mortimer).

For in what stupid age or nation,
Was marriage ever out of fashion? (Samuel Butler).

Don't let your marriage go stale. Change the bag on the Hoover of life (Victoria Wood).

Marriage is the only adventure open to the cowardly (Voltaire).

Why does a woman work ten years to change a man's habits and then complain that he's not the man she married? (Barbra Streisand).

It has been said that a bride's attitude towards her betrothed can be summed up by three words associated with weddings: Aisle, altar, hymn (Anon).

Her husband made her happy by adding some magic to their marriage . . . he disappeared (Nicholas Murray Butler).

When a girl marries she exchanges the attentions of many men for the inattention of one (Helen Rowland).

You live in your heart, so you have to be very careful about what you put there (Marti Caine).

A daughter's a daughter for all of her life, but a son is a son till he gets a wife (Anon).

In the arithmetic of love, one plus one equals everything and two minus one equals nothing (Mignon McLaughlin).

Two can live as cheaply as one, and after marriage they do (Anon).

Nowadays two can live as cheaply as one large family used to (Joey Adams).

A happy marriage is the union of two good forgivers (Robert Quillen).

True love is like the misty rain that falls so softly, yet floods the river (Nigerian proverb).

Marriage teaches you loyalty, forbearance, self-restraint and many other qualities you wouldn't need if you stayed single (Anon).

A ring on the finger is worth two on the phone (Harold Thomson).

Two souls with but a single thought,
Two hearts that beat as one (Maria Lovell).

Marriage is our last, best chance to grow up (Joseph Barth).

Let there be spaces in your togetherness (Kahalil Gibran).

When you are in love, you tell each other a thousand things without talking (Hawaiian proverb).

Let's get married . . . It's a piece of paper but it says, 'I love you' (The Proclaimers, *Let's Get Married*).

Love is like a curry and I'll explain to you,
That love comes in three temperatures: medium, hot and vindaloo (Pam Ayres).

I will never marry because I could never be satisfied with any woman stupid enough to have me (Abraham Lincoln).

If you would have a happy family life, remember two things: in matters of principle, stand like a rock; in matters of taste, swim with the current (Thomas Jefferson).

The heart can do anything (French proverb).

A good husband should be deaf and a good wife blind (French proverb).

Some people ask the secret of our long marriage. We take time to go out to a restaurant two times a week. A little candlelight, dinner, soft music and dancing. She goes Tuesday, I go Fridays (Henry Youngman).

It takes two to make a marriage a success and only one a failure (Herbert Samuel).

Don't let's ask for the moon. We have the stars! (Bette Davis to Paul Henreid in *Now Voyager*).

Married couples resemble a pair of scissors, often moving in opposite directions, yet always punishing anyone who comes between them (Sydney Smith).

Every man needs a wife because things sometimes go wrong that you can't blame on the government (Anon).

Like the measles, love is most dangerous when it comes late in life (Lord Byron).

Actually, I believe in marriage, having done it several times (Joan Collins).

Second marriage: the triumph of hope over experience (Samuel Johnson).

Zsa Zsa Gabor got married as a one-off and it was so successful she turned it into a series (Bob Hope).

I'm not so old, and not so plain, and I'm quite prepared to marry again (W.S. Gilbert – useful for second marriages).

Love and marriage,
Love and marriage,
Go together like a horse and carriage. (Popular song by Sammy Cahn – particularly apt if the couple travelled by horse and carriage.)

Marriage is an armed alliance against the outside world (G.K. Chesterton).

The most beautiful things in the world cannot be seen or even touched. They must be felt with the heart (Helen Keller).

Everything I do I do it for you (Record-breaking No. 1 hit by Bryan Adams).

Love is like a curry. You really have to have confidence in it to enjoy it (Mike Smith).

A woman is like a tea bag – you don't know her strength until she is in hot water (Nancy Reagan).

Mary and I have been married for 47 years, and not once have we ever had an argument serious enough to mention the word divorce . . . murder, yes, but divorce, never (Jack Benny).

I belong to Bridegrooms Anonymous. Whenever I feel like getting married they send over a lady in a housecoat and hair curlers to burn my toast for me (Dick Martin).

I am feeling very lonely. I've been married for 15 years, and yesterday my wife ran off with the chap next door. I'm going to miss him terribly (Les Dawson).

I don't for the life of me understand why people keep insisting marriage is doomed. All five of mine worked out (Peter De Vries).

I'm the only man who has a marriage licence made out 'To Whom It May Concern' (Mickey Rooney).

Marriage turns a night owl into a homing pigeon (Glenn Shelton).

Most girls seem to marry men who happen to be like their fathers. Maybe that's why so many mothers cry at weddings (Jenny Eclair).

Marriage is like wine. It gets better with age (Dudley Moore).

Love is the answer and you know that for sure (John Lennon).

When I proposed, I said, 'I offer you my hand, my heart and my washing' (A.A. Milne).

Marriage: a strong union which defies management (Will Rogers).

It was a beautiful wedding – one of my better ones (Jim Davidson).

Woman begins by resisting man's advances and ends by blocking his retreat (Oscar Wilde).

I never married because there was no need. I have three pets at home which answer the same purpose as a husband. I have a dog which growls every morning, a parrot which swears all the afternoon and a cat that comes home late at night (Marie Corelli).

Getting married is like getting a dog. It teaches you to be less self-centred, to expect sudden, surprising outbursts of affection, and not to be upset by a few scratches on your car (Will Stanton).

Love is like quicksilver in the hand. Leave the fingers open and it stays; clutch it, and it darts away (Dorothy Parker).

Laugh and the world laughs with you, snore and you sleep alone (Anthony Burgess).

4
Naming Names

An excellent way to make a speech unique and memorable is to refer to the original meaning of the couple's names. Your reference could be humorous or serious or perhaps both. For example:

> The other day, for a bit of fun, I looked up the meaning of the happy couple's first names. They are very appropriate. Donna comes from the Italian word for lady. And who could argue with that description? The name Philip comes from the Greek for horse-loving. And that must be true as well, because Phil has been known to make the occasional visit to Ladbrokes.

> The name Jeffrey comes from the German for joyful. How appropriate, because I'm sure Jeff is now the happiest man in the world. The name Claire comes from the Latin for shining brightly. How true; doesn't she look radiant?

Here are charts of Top 100 names given to both boys and girls born in England and Wales between 1965 and 1980. Where there are variations in spelling (Alan, Allan and Allen), the most popular version is given. For convenience, the names are listed alphabetically, not in order of popularity, using these abbreviations:

Aram., Aramaic; Celt., Celtic; Fr., French; Gael., Gaelic; Ger., German; Gk., Greek; Hb., Hebrew; Ir., Irish; It., Italian; Lt., Latin; O.E., Old English.

TOP 100 BOYS' NAMES 1965–80

Aaron Hb. High mountain
Adam Hb. Red skin
Adrian Lt. Of the Adriatic
Alan Celt. Of a nomadic tribe
Alexander Gk. Defender of men
Alistair Gk. Defender of men
Andrew Gk. Manly

59

Anthony Lt. Praiseworthy
Ashley O.E. Ash wood
Barry Ir. A spear
Ben Hb. The right hand
Benjamin Hb. The right hand
Brendan Gael. Stinking hair
Brian Celt. Strong
Carl Ger. Free man
Charles Ger. Free man
Christian Lt. Christian
Christopher Gk. Carrying Christ
Clive O.E. Lives by the cliff
Colin O.E. A peasant
Craig O.E. Of the rocks
Damian Gk. To tame
Daniel Hb. God is my judge
Darren Ir. (From an Irish surname)
Darryl (From Airel, Normandy)
David Hb. Beloved
Dean O.E. Valley dweller
Dennis Gk. (After the God of
    fertility and wine)
Derek Ger. Ruler of the people
Edward O.E. Happy guardian
Gareth Celt. Old man
Gary Fr. Warrior rule
Gavin Celt. White hawk
Geoffrey Ger. Peace
Glenn Gael. Lives in the valley
Graham O.E. Granta's place
Gregory Gk. Watchful
Ian Gael. God's mercy
Jacob Hb. One who takes over
James Hb. One who takes over
Jamie Hb. One who takes over
Jared Hb. Rose
Jason Hb. Healer
Jeffrey Ger. Joyful
Jeremy Hb. Jehovah exalts
John Hb. God's mercy
Jonathan Hb. God's gift

Joseph Hb. Addition to the family
Joshua Hb. God is salvation
Julian Lt. Soft-haired
Justin Lt. Just
Keith Celt. Wood
Kenneth Gael. Born of fire
Kevin Celt. Handsome
Kieran Gael. Little dark one
Kyle Gael. Narrow
Lawrence Lt. From Laurentum
    (nr Rome)
Lee O.E. Wood
Liam Gael. Defender
Luke Gk. From Lucania (S. Italy)
Malcolm Gael. Follower of
    St Columba
Marcus Lt. A hammer
Mark Lt. A hammer
Martin Lt. War-like
Matthew Hb. God's gift
Michael Hb. Who is like God?
Nathan Hb. God has given
Neil Gael. Champion
Nicholas Gk. Victory of the
    people
Nigel Lt. Black
Oliver Fr. Olive tree
Patrick Lt. A nobleman
Paul Lt. Small
Peter Gk. A rock
Philip Gk. Horse-loving
Raymond Ger. Wise protection
Richard Ger. Strong ruler
Robert Ger. Bright flame
Robin O.E. Bright flame
Roger Fr. Fame spear (Famous
    spearman)
Ross Gael. Headland
Russell Fr. Little red one
Ryan Gael. King
Samuel Hb. Name of God

Scott (Moved from Ireland to Scotland)
Shane Gael. God's mercy
Shaun Hb. God's mercy
Simon Gk. Snub-nosed
Stacey Fr. Good harvest
Stephen Gk. A crown
Stuart O.E. A steward
Terry Ger. Tribe power
Thomas Aram. Twin
Timothy Gk. Honoured by God
Todd O.E. Fox
Trevor Celt. Big village
Troy Fr. From Troyes, France
Warren Fr. From La Varenne, France
Wayne O.E. Waggon-maker
William Ger. Defender

TOP 100 GIRLS' NAMES 1965–80

Abigail Hb. Father rejoices
Alexandra Gk. Defender of men
Alison Ger. Noble
Amanda Lt. Lovable
Amy Fr. Loved
Andrea Feminine form of *Andrew* Gk. Manly
Angela Gk. Messenger
Ann Hb. Fortunate
Anna Hb. Fortunate
Ashley O.E. Ash wood
Beverley O.E. Beaver stream
Carla Ger. Free person
Carly Ger. Free person
Carol Ger. Noble-spirited
Caroline Ger. Noble-spirited
Catherine Gk. Pure
Charlene Ger. Free person
Charlotte Fr. Free person

Christine Fr. Christian
Claire Lt. Shining brightly
Danielle Hb. God is judge
Dawn Lt. Dawn
Deborah Hb. A bee
Denise Gk. (After the God of fertility and wine)
Diane Lt. Divine
Donna It. A lady
Elaine Gk. Light
Elizabeth Hb. God's oath
Emily Lt. (After a Roman surname)
Emma Ger. Universal
Fiona Gael. Fair
Gemma It. Jewel
Gillian Lt. Soft-haired
Hannah Hb. God has favoured me
Hayley O.E. Hay field
Heather O.E. Heather
Helen Gk. Light
Jacqueline Lt. One who takes over
Jane Lt. God's mercy
Janet Hb. God's mercy
Jenna Celt. White-cheeked
Jennifer Celt. White-cheeked
Jessica Hb. God beholds
Joanna Hb. God's mercy
Joanne Hb. God's mercy
Jodie Hb. Jewess
Julie Lt. Soft-haired
Karen Gk. Pure
Kate Gk. Pure
Katharine Gk. Pure
Katie Gk. Pure
Kayleigh Gael. Slender
Kelly Celt. War-like
Kerry Gael. (After the Irish county)

Kimberley O.E. (After the S. African town)
Kirsty Gael. Christian
Laura Lt. Laurel
Lauren Lt. From Laurentum (nr Rome)
Leah Hb. Languid
Leanne (Lee O.E. Wood; Ann Hb. Fortunate)
Lesley Gael. Garden of hollies
Linda Ger. A snake
Lindsay O.E. Wetland of Lincoln
Lisa Hb. God's oath
Lorraine Fr. (Joan of Arc's surname)
Louise Ger. Famous warrior
Lucy Lt. Light
Lynn O.E. Brook
Mandy Lt. Lovable
Margaret Gk. Pearl
Maria Lt. Star of the sea
Marie Lt. Star of the sea
Melanie Gk. Black
Melissa Gk. A bee
Michelle Hb. Who is God?
Natalie Lt. Christmas Day
Natasha Lt. Christmas Day
Nicola Gk. Victory of the people
Paula Lt. Small
Rachel Hb. A ewe
Rebecca Hb. Charmer
Sally Hb. Princess
Samantha Aram. Listener
Sandra Hb. Defender
Sarah Hb. Princess
Sharon Hb. (A biblical place name)
Sophie Gk. Wisdom
Stacey Fr. Good harvest
Stephanie Gk. A crown
Susan Hb. A lily

Suzanne Hb. A lily
Tammy Hb. Date palm
Teresa Gk. Reaper
Tina O.E. Christian
Tracey Gk. Reaper
Vicki Lt. Conquerer
Victoria Lt. Conquerer
Wendy (After a character in *Peter Pan*)
Yvonne Fr. Yew tree
Zoë Gk. Life

WELSH NAMES

Most children born in England or Wales between 1965 and 1980 have one of these 200 first names. However, in some parts of Wales – notably throughout the north and west of the Principality – other names are even more popular. Here are one hundred of them.

50 popular Welsh boys' names

Aled (After the river)
Alun Of a nomadic tribe
Arwyn/Awen Muse
Bleddyn Wolf
Bryn Hill
Brynmor Great hill
Cadwaladr Leader in battle
Caradoc Love
Carwyn Blessed love
Cemlyn Bent lake
Ceri Love
Cledwyn (After the river)
Dafydd Beloved
Deinol Charming
Dewi Beloved

Dyfan Ruler of the tribe
Dylan Son of the waves
Edryd Restoration
Eifion (After the place)
Eilir Butterfly
Elfed Autumn
Elgan Bright circle
Elis Yahweh (Jehova) is God
Elwyn White brow
Emrys Immortal
Emyr Honour
Eryl Watcher
Euros Gold
Geraint Old
Gethin Dusky
Glyndwr Valley of water
Gruffydd Powerful chief
Gwilym Defender
Gwyn Blessed
Gwynfor Fair lord
Hefin Summery
Heilyn Steward
Huw Mind
Iestyn Just
Ieuan/Ifan/Iwan God's mercy
Iolo/Iorwerth Handsome lord
Melfyn From Carmarthen
Morgan Great and bright
Owain Well born
Pryderi Caring for
Rhodri Circle-ruler
Rhys Ardour
Sion God's mercy
Trefor Big village
Wyn Pure

50 popular Welsh girls' names
Angharad Much loved
Anwen Very beautiful
Arwenna Muse

Bethan God's oath
Blodwen White flowers
Bronwen White breast
Carys Love
Ceinwen Lovely and blessed
Ceridwen Holy poetry
Cerys Love
Delyth Pretty
Dilys Genuine
Eirlys Snowdrop
Eirwen White snow
Elen Angel
Eleri (After the river)
Elin Nymph
Enfys Rainbow
Ffion Foxglove
Ffraid The high one
Gaenor White and smooth
Gladys Lame
Glenda Pure and good
Glenys Pure
Gwen Blessed
Gwendolen Holy ring
Gwyneth Happiness
Heulwen Sunshine
Lora Laurel
Lowri Laurel
Mai Pearl
Mair Star of the sea
Mared Pearl
Mari Star of the sea
Megan Star of the sea
Meinwen Slender and blessed
Meironwen White dairymaid
Mererid Star of the sea
Meriel Bright sea
Myfanwy My fine one
Nerys Lord
Nesta Pure
Olwen White footprint
Rhiain Maiden

Rhiannon Goddess
Rhonwen Fair-haired
Sian God's mercy
Sioned God's mercy
Tegwen Fair and blessed
Tirion Gentle

SCOTTISH AND IRISH NAMES

Similarly, the following four sets of names are particularly popular throughout Scotland and Ireland. Some of these Gaelic names are used in both countries, often with slight variations of spelling.

50 popular Scottish boys' names

Adair Prosperity spear
Adie/Adaidh Red skin
Alasdair Defending men
Alpin White
Angus Unique choice
Archibald Genuine and brave
Aulay Ancestor
Barclay Wood or birches
Broderick Brother
Calum Dove
Cameron Crooked nose
Campbell Crooked mouth
Conall Strong wolf
Conan Hound
Diarmad Envy free
Donald/Domhnall World rule
Dougal/Dugald Dark stranger
Duncan/Donnchad Brown battle
Erskine Green ascent
Ewan Well born

Farquhar Very dear one
Fergus Supreme choice
Finlay Fair hero
Forbes Field or district
Gillespie Bishop's servant
Gillies Servant of Jesus
Grant Large
Gregor/Greg/Griogair Watchful
Hamish/Seumas One who takes over
Ia(i)n God's mercy
Keir A fort
Kirk A church
Lachlan Fjord-land (from Norway)
Leslie Garden of hollies
Ludovic Famous in battle
Magnus Great
Maxwell Mack's stream
Mungo Amiable
Murdo/Murchadh/Murdoch The sea
Murray From Moray
Rab/Rabbie/Rob Bright flame
Ramsay Wild garlic island
Ri(t)chie Strong ruler
Rory Red-haired
Ross Headland
Rowan Red
Sandy/Sawney Defending men
Seaghdh/Shaw Hawk-like
Sholto/Sioltach Seed-bearing
Wallace Foreign or Celtic

50 popular Scottish girls' names

Ailsa (After the rock, Ailsa Craig)
Alana Member of a nomadic tribe
Alexina Defender of men
Antonia Praiseworthy

Beathag Life
Calumina/Mina Dove
Catriona Pure
Christy Christian
Ciorstaidh Christian
Davina Beloved
Deoiridh/Dorcas Pilgrim
Dolina World rule
Donella World rule
Ealasaid God's oath
Edme Love
Edwina Rich friend
Efric/Oighrig New speckled one
Eilidh/Ailie Light
Elspeth/Elsie God's oath
Esme Esteemed
Eubh Lively
Fenella/Fionnghal White
  shoulder
Flora Flower
Freya Lady
Georgina A farmer
Gormlaith/Gormelia Illustrious
  lady
Greer Watchful
Innes Island
Iona (After the island)
Iseabail/Ishbel God's oath
Isla (After the river)
Jeanie God's mercy
Jessie/Teasag God's mercy
Katrine (After the loch)
Lorna (After Lorn, nr Oban)
Maili/Mairi Star of the sea
Malvina Smooth brow
Mor/Morag Princess
Morna Beloved
Morven Big mountain peak
Peigi Pearl
Rhona Rough island
Senga Slender

Sheena/Sine God's mercy
Shona/Seonaird God's mercy
Siubhan God's mercy
Siusan A lily
Stineag Christian
Teasag Gift
Thora Dedicated to Thor

50 popular Irish boys' names
Aodh/Aodan/Aidan Fire
Ard(gh)al High valour
Brendan Stinking hair
Calum/Cally Dove
Cathal Battle mighty
Cian/Kean(e) Ancient
Ciaran Black
Conleth Chief lord
Connor/Conn Lover of hounds
Cormac Charioteer
Cornelius Horn
Daley Gathering
Declan (After the fifth century
  saint)
Dermot Without envy
Desmond From south Munster
Donagh/Dono(u)gh Brown battle
Donal World rule
Donn Brown
Donovan Brown and black
Duane/Dubhan Black
Eamonn Rich protector
Enda Bird
Eoghan Well born
Eoin God's mercy
Fergal Man of valour
Finbar/Fionnb(h)arr Fair
  headed
Finn/Fionn Fair
Flannan Of ruddy complexion
Florry/Flurry Leader and king
Garrett Firm spear

Loughlin Fjord-land (from Norway)
Manus Great
Niall Champion
Nioclas Victory of the people
Oran/Odhran Shallow
Osheen/Oisin Deer
Padraig/Paraic/Porick Nobleman
Redmond Counsel and protector
Risteard Strong ruler
Roibeard Bright flame
Ronan A seal (the animal)
Rory/Ruaidhri Red haired
Seamas/Seumus Heel
Sean God's messenger
Se(a)nan Wise
Tadgh/Tad/Teague Philosopher
Tarlach Instigator
Tomas Twin
Tuathal/Toal Ruler of a tribe

50 popular Irish girls' names

Aine Radiance
Aisling/Ashling Vision
Aoibheann/Eavan Beautiful
Aoife Beauty
Attracta/Athracht Drawn to
Bernadette Brave
Bridget The high one
Caitlin/Caitriona/Triona Pure
Ciara Black
Clodagh (After the Tipperary river)
Deirdre The broken-hearted
Donla Brown lady
Dorean/Doireann Finn's daughter
Dymphna/Damhnait Fawn
Eabha Alive

Edna/Et(h)na/Ena/Eithne Kernel
Eileen/Eibhlin Light
Eilis God's oath
Fiona/Fina Fair
Grainne Disgust
Ita Thirst
Kayley Slender
Keeley/Keelin Slender and white
Lean Light
Maeve/Mave/Meave Intoxicating
Mairead Pearl
Mairin/Maureen Wished-for child
Majella (After St Gerard Majella)
Maura Star of the sea
Muirne/Myrna/Morna Beloved
Napla Lovable
Niamh Bright
Noreen Honourable
Nuala White shoulder
Oona/Una Unity
Orla Golden lady
Patsy Of noble birth
Paudeen Of noble birth
Raghnailt Queen
Roisin Rose
Sabia/Sadhbh/Sabina/Sive Sweet
Saoirse Freedom
Sheila/Sile Blind
Sibeal God's oath
Sinead God's mercy
Siobhan/Chevonne God's mercy
Sorcha Bright
Talulla/Tuilelaith Abundant princess
Treasa To reap
Whiltierna/Faoiltiarna Wolf lord

MUSLIM AND HINDU NAMES

As Britain is a multi-cultural society it is useful to know the meanings of some of the most popular names throughout the Arab world and across the Indian subcontinent. Because of the unifying influence of Islam, names tend to be very similar throughout the entire Arab world. And unlike Western names, which are largely borrowed from other languages, they are original and their meanings can usually be found in a dictionary. So here are 100 popular Muslim names, together with their English translations.

50 popular boys' names throughout the Arab world

Abbas Austere
Abd-al- — Servant of the —
Adil Just
Adnan To settle down
Ahmad More commendable
Ali Sublime
Amin Trustworthy
Ayman Prosperous
Aziz Invincible
Badr Full moon
Bakr Young camel
Fadil Generous
Fahd Leopard
Faruq Knowing what's right
Faysal A judge
Ghassan Prime of youth
Ghayth Rain
Hadi Leader
Hamdi Praise and thanks
Hamid Thankful
Harith Provider
Hasan Beautiful
Hasim/Hatim Decisive
Haythan Young eagle
Husam Sword
Husayn Beautiful
Khalid Eternal
Khayrat Good deed
Khayri Charitable
Mahir Skilful
Mahmud Praiseworthy
Majid Glorious
Mamduh Praised
Mansur Victorious
Mazin Rain clouds
Midhat Praise
Muhammad Praiseworthy
Mustafa Chosen
Omar/Umar Flourishing
Qusay Remote
Rashad Good sense
Salah Righteousness
Samir Night talk
Tahir Pure
Talal Fine rain
Tariq Night visitor
Usama Lion
Uthman Baby bustard
Wasim Handsome
Zayd To increase
Zuhayr Flowers

50 popular girls' names throughout the Arab world

Abir Fragrance
Abla Fine figured
Ahlam Dreams
Aisha Alive and well

Amina Peaceful
Arwa Mountain goat
Asma Prestige
Azza Pride
Bahiyya Beautiful
Buthayna Good land
Dalal Coquettishness
Dalia Dahlia
Dima Downpour
Fatima Abstainer
Fatin Charming
Fayruz Turquoise (precious stone)
Fidda Silver
Ghada Graceful girl
Ghadir Stream
Hadil Cooing of pigeons
Hadya Leader
Hajar To emigrate
Hayfa Slender
Huda Right guidance
Isra Night journey
Jathibiyya Charm
Khadija Premature child
Khayriyya Charitable
Layla Wine
Lubna A storax tree
Lujayn Silver
Madiha Praise
Malak Angel
Marwa Fragrant plant
Muna Hope
Nada Morning dew
Nadya Moist with dew
Nahla A drink of water
Nihal Thirst quenched
Rabab Musical instrument
Rana Beautiful
Rim White antelope
Sabah Morning
Samar/Samira Night talk

Sawsan Lily of the valley
Shahrazad City person
Thana Praise
Thurayya The Pleiades
Zahra Blossom
Zaynab Fragrant plant

Islamic influences are strong in India, and especially in Pakistan and Bangladesh. And as most personal names borne by Muslims are Arabic, many will be found above. However, about three quarters of the population of the Indian subcontinent speak languages derived from Sanskrit. So here are 100 popular Hindu names based on this classic literary language, together with their meanings.

50 popular boys' names throughout the Indian sub-continent

Amitabh Of unmeasured splendour
Amrit Immortal
Anil Air
Arjun White
Arvind/Aravind/Aurobindo Lotus
Bharat Being maintained
Chandra/Candra/Chander Shining moon
Devdan/Deodan/Debdan Gift of the gods
Dilip/Duleep Defender of Delhi
Dipak/Deepak Little lamp
Ganesh/Gowri Lord of the hosts
Gopal Cowherd

Gotam/Gautam The best ox
Indra Having rain drops
Jagannath Lord of the world
Kalidas The black one
Kamal Pale-red
Kapil Reddish-brown
Karan Ear
Kasi Shining
Krishna/Kishen/Kistna/Kannan Dark
Madhav Of the spring
Mahavir Great hero
Mani Jewel
Murali Flute
Nanda Joy
Narendra/Narender A mighty man
Nataraj King of dancers
Padma Lotus
Prabhakar Illuminator
Radha Success
Raj/Raja/Rajan/Rajam King
Rajendra/Rajender Mighty king
Rajiv Striped
Rama/Ram/Ramu Pleasing
Ratan/Ratnam Jewel
Samant Universal
Sanjay Triumphant
Shankar/Sankar Auspicious
Shiva/Sib/Sheo Auspicious
Surya Sun
Tara Saviour
Tulsi Holy basil
Vasant/Basant Spring
Vasu/Basu Bright
Venkat A sacred hill
Vijay/Bijay/Bijoy Victory
Vikram Pace
Vishnu/Bishen The god Vishnu
Vishwanath Lord of all

50 popular girls' names throughout the Indian sub-continent

Aruna/Aravind Reddish-brown
Bala Young
Chandra/Candra/Chander Shining moon
Devi Goddess
Devika Little goddess
Gauri/Gowri White
Gita/Geeta Song
Indira Beauty
Jaya Victory
Jyoti Light
Kalpana Fantasy
Kamala Pale-red
Kanta Desired
Kishori Filly
Kumari Daughter
Lakshmi/Laxmi Sign
Lalita/Lalit Playful
Leela/Lila Play
Madhav Of the spring
Madhu Honey
Madhur Sweet
Mohana/Mohini Bewitching
Parvati Daughter of the mountain
Padmavati Full of lotuses
Pratibha Light
Purnima Night of full moon
Radha Success
Rajalakshmi Goddess of fortune
Rajani The dark one
Rati Rest
Rukmini Adorned with gold
Rupinder Of greatest beauty
Sandhya Twilight
Saraswati Lake
Sarojini Having lotuses
Shanta Calm

Shanti Tranquility
Sharada Autumnal
Sharmila Modest
Sheela Conduct
Shobhana Beautiful
Shyama Dark
Sita/Seeta/Seetha Furrow
Sru/Shree/Shri Prosperity

Sujata Of noble birth
Sumati Intelligent
Sunita/Suniti Of good
    conduct
Sushila/Susheela Good-
    tempered
Usha Dawn
Vimala Pure

In this chapter we have considered the meanings of over 700 of the most popular first names in the UK. However, if either the bride's or groom's name isn't listed you should find it in one of the specialist names books listed under 'Further Reading' at the back of this book.

Sometimes you can use a name as the basis of a joke or good line. But be very careful not to be offensive or childish. Here is a good joke for an Alexander, Alfred, Catherine or Fredrick:

> Lucy told me that she will always respect Alexander and she will show her respect. As they sit before an open fire on a cold winter evening, and another log is needed, she will turn to her beloved and say, 'Alexander, the grate'.

SURNAMES

So much for first names. It is often possible also to make some interesting reference to surnames. Although there are hundreds of thousands of different surnames throughout Britain, rather surprisingly, according to the 1990 *National Population Census*, the Top 50 of them account for over 12 million Britons – over one-fifth of the population. And when the surnames which relate directly to these 50 key surnames are taken into account (for example, Arrowsmith, Goldsmith, Smithe, Smithies, Smithson, Smythe and many, many others all relate directly to the number one name – Smith), over 40% of the entire population is included. So here is an alphabetical chart of the top 50 surnames throughout England and Wales in the 1990s.

Celt., Celtic; Gk., Greek; Hb., Hebrew; Lt., Latin; O.E., Old English; O.F., Old French; O.G., Old German.

Top 50 surnames in England and Wales

Allan/Allen O.F. Of a nomadic tribe
Bailey O.F. Bailiff
Baker O.F. Baker
Bennett Lt. Blessed
Brown O.E. Brown-haired
Carter O.E. Maker or driver of carts
Clark(e) O.E. Cleric or secretary
Cook O.E. Cook or seller of cooked meat
Cooper O.E. Barrel maker
Davi(e)s O.F. Son of Davy
Edwards O.E. Guardian of happiness
Evans Celt. Son of Evan
Green O.E. Lives by village green
Griffiths Lt. Red-haired
Hall O.E. Works at the manor
Harris(on) O.G. Ruler of the house
Hill O.E. Lives on the hill
Hughes O.E. Son of Hugh
Jackson O.E. Son of Jack
James Hb. One who takes over
Johnson O.E. Son of John
Jones O.E. Son of John
King O.E. King (ran village pageants)
Lee O.E. Clearing or pasture
Lewis O.G. Famous in battle
Martin Lt. War-like
Moore O.F. Dark complexion
Morgan Celt. Sea-bright
Morris O.F. Dark complexion
Parker O.F. Park keeper or ranger
Phillips Gk. Son of Philip
Price Celt. Son of Rhys
Richardson O.E. Son of Richard
Robert(son) O.G. Bright flame
Robinson O.F. Son of Robert
Scott Lt. (From Ireland to Scotland)
Smith O.E. Metal worker
Taylor O.E. Tailor
Thomas O.F. Twin
Thompson O.F. Twin
Turner O.F. Works with a lathe
Walker O.E. Cloth worker
Ward O.E. Guard or watchman
Watson O.E. Son of Walter
White O.E. White complexion
Williams O.E. Son of William
Wilson O.E. Son of Will
Wood O.E. Lives in the wood
Wright O.E. Carpenter or joiner
Young O.E. Young or junior

However it is not always necessary to refer to the original meaning of a surname. For example, any newly married Mr Robinson would be missing a golden opportunity if he did not say something like:

As Simon and Garfunkel toasted Anne Bancroft in *The Graduate*, 'And here's to you, Mrs Robinson'!

And if your name happens to be Mr or Mrs Wright – well the possibilities are endless.

5
Anecdotes and Jokes

An anecdote (a short personal story) or a joke can really lift a speech and make it individual and memorable. Choose your material very carefully. It must be in keeping with your own personality, the tone of your speech and the expectations of your audience. It must also be original. Don't repeat any story or joke which you recently heard on television because Murphy's Law tells us that at least one other person in the room will have been watching the same programme. Similarly, don't tell one that has already been aired at a previous family gathering. Finally, don't get carried away – you are not a stand-up comedian.

THREE GOOD RULES FOR STORY-TELLING

Never use any material unless you are sure it conforms to the 3R rule of story-telling. A joke or anecdote must be:

- Relevant
- Realistic
- Retellable.

Relevant
Your story must be *meaningful* to your audience. You may know a wonderful gag about a window cleaner and an MP. Even if it is the funniest story in the world, don't tell it unless the bride, groom or best man is a window cleaner, or an MP. In this chapter you will find several anecdotes and jokes about various jobs and hobbies. You will also find some good jokes and lines that would be particularly useful in each of the main speeches.

Realistic
Your story doesn't have to be true, but it should sound as it if *could* be true. Reg Smythe, the cartoonist responsible for the long-running *Andy Capp* strip, says, 'Never draw anything that hasn't happened or couldn't

happen.' The same principle applies to making a speech: you should never talk about anything that hasn't happened or couldn't happen. So it is fine to talk about a man with three hats, but not about a man with three heads.

Retellable

'Something old, something new, something borrowed, something blue.' That is what a bride is supposed to have about her on her wedding day. The first three things – something old, something new and something borrowed – also apply to the contents of a good speech. The fourth – something blue – most certainly does *not*.

GETTING IT RIGHT

Aim to be amusing but never risqué. A little flippancy is fine but don't say anything offensive or cynical. To say, 'Marriage isn't a word, it's a sentence' is a great line for a stand-up comedian but not for a wedding speech. This is the bride's day and no one should say a word against her or the institution of marriage. So while a little crack about her job or hobby is fine, there must be absolutely no reference to sex, pregnancy, the honeymoon, or to any previous relationships. Also, try to include a joke or two against yourself. Audiences love speakers who don't take themselves too seriously. Before you tell a story or crack a joke, ask yourself whether it passes this test which Bob Monkhouse devised for all his potential material:

1. Do *you* think it is funny?
2. Can you say it confidently and with comfort?
3. Is there any danger of offending anyone?
4. Will they understand and appreciate it?

Do *you* think it is funny?

If you're not really happy about a joke or story you will not tell it confidently. Not only that, your audience probably won't find it funny either. Professional gagsters follow this maxim: If in doubt, leave it out. So should you.

Can you say it confidently and with comfort?

Stick to the KISS principle: Keep It Short and Simple. Avoid any long or complicated stories, difficult words or phrases and anything requiring regional or national accents. And ask yourself: Is this story right for *me*?

A twenty-year-old should not tell a story about his silver wedding anniversary.

Is there any danger of offending anyone?

Avoid anything racist, sexist, or ageist, and steer well clear of politics, religion, sex and disabilities. In short, use your common sense. Remember: If in doubt, leave it out.

Will they understand and appreciate it?

Your audience may be aged anything between 3 and 93 and they will probably have a very wide range of backgrounds. So it is impossible to give a speech totally suited to everyone present. However, what you can do is avoid the extremes of, on the one hand, telling childish jokes and, on the other hand, telling complicated, technical stories comprehensible only to a professor of applied nuclear physics. Also avoid in-jokes; they are a real turn-off for those not in the know. Finally, remember that some jokes which are really funny when *read*, can be totally incomprehensible when *heard*. This can illustrated by the following:

> Chris isn't a great reader so I was surprised to find a tattered volume of an out-of-date encyclopaedia in his room. When I saw the letters on the side of the volume I laughed at the thought of what must have been his utter surprise and shattering disappointment when he first got the book home. The letters read: 'HOW to HUG'.

You can *see* how this amusing confusion was caused, but you would not have easily appreciated it if you had *heard* the gag. (Its punchline: 'The letters read: H-O-W to H-U-G' would have sounded like double Dutch to you.) So the moral is clear: always rehearse your speech *out loud*, preferably in front of a small audience or on videotape. Then if something doesn't work – as this one certainly wouldn't have – take it out.

ADAPTING AND PERSONALISING MATERIAL

Once you are satisfied that a joke or anecdote passes the 3R test of story-telling and the Monkhouse Test, you will need to adapt it, that is make a few changes here and there until it is *meaningful* to your audience. For example, if you want to tell a story about a taxi driver you might well be able to adapt one about a bus driver or a lorry driver. Any gag involving motor vehicles or a long road journey could probably apply to any of them.

Then you must personalise your material. Don't tell a story about a taxi driver – any old taxi driver – tell one about a particular taxi driver, probably about the bride, the bridegroom or best man. Don't talk about 'a town', mention *your* town. And don't say 'he drove down a back street', say 'Don drove down Inkerman Street'. In other words, give your audience enough local details so they can actually see the events as you describe them – if only in their minds' eye.

Funnily enough, a teasing little joke and a sincere compliment often fit in very well together. For example,

Helen recently joined the string section of the town orchestra. She practises at home day and night. She's always harping on about something or other [pause]. Well, angels do, don't they?

Here's another example:

When I asked Ian about all the wedding arrangements he said, 'Oh, I'll leave all that to you. But I do want Bells – and at least three cases of it' [pause]. Well I don't know about Bells, but I work with Ian at Grange Hill Comprehensive – and I can tell you that he is certainly one of the best Teachers I know.

And how about this sort of thing for the sporty types?

Boris practises by hitting a tennis ball against his garage door. It's really improved his game. He hasn't won yet, but last week he took the door to five sets [pause]. No, Boris and Martina are both excellent tennis players – the perfect match.

So try to sugar your jokes with praise.

PAUSING

You will have noticed that I have suggested where you pause to get your laughs. Usually this is obvious. It's all about timing. If the guests clap or cheer (even if you weren't expecting it), pause. If you tell a serious or sentimental story, pause for a second or two to let the moral sink in. However, if a joke falls flat, as soon as you realise it get straight on – make it seem as if no laughs were expected. Never, never repeat a joke or punchline, or say anything like 'You're slow today', or 'Don't you get it?' – that makes it look like you are begging for a positive reaction. If it's funny they'll laugh, if it's not they won't.

Right, here are some anecdotes and jokes about various jobs and hobbies, followed by some more general little stories, gags and other lines particularly suited to each of the main speeches. Choose one or two relevant ones, adapt and personalise them, and tell them using your own words. Or, better still, try to think of original ones yourself. If they happen to be true, or at least are based on truth, then so much the better.

JOBS

Some stories and gags could apply to *any* job, for example:

Matthew's boss says he's a miracle worker. It's a miracle if he works.

Justin asked me to give his application form a quick once over before he sent it off. It was a good thing he did. Where he was asked, 'Length of residence at present address', he had replied, 'About 20 metres – not counting the garage'.

I asked Tina how many people work at Matthew and Son. 'About half', she replied.

Pat has a perfect attendance record. He's never missed a tea break.

When Andy left Bloggs Ltd, they gave him this reference: 'Any employer who gets Mr Capp to work for him will be very lucky'.

However, it is far better if you refer to someone's actual job and to the name of the company they work for.

With a little thought, many of the following gags can be adapted for other occupations as well.

Accountant/stockbroker
Little Jimmy asked Donny what 2 + 2 came to. Donny looked him in the eye and replied, 'That depends on whether you are buying or selling'.

Antiques shop/art gallery/auction room/museum curator
On his first day at Acorn Antiques, Sandy dropped a priceless vase. Julian, his new boss, was in more tears than this cake. 'That was over 400 years old,' he cried. 'Lucky it wasn't a new one,' said Sandy.

Architect/draughtsman
Every morning, as Tom leaves for work he says, 'Ah, well, back to the drawing board.'

Bank/Building Society
A bank is a place where they lend you an umbrella in fine weather and ask for it back when it begins to rain.

British Telecom/Mercury employee
Julie, why are wrong numbers never engaged?

Builder/electrician/handyman/plumber/etc.
You all know that Dean is a builder, but what you probably don't know is that he is also an excellent story-teller. When he tells a customer that he'll be there at 8 he will be more likely to turn up at 10. Anyway, today he is going to give us a speech and that will be the first time he has ever finished something on the same day that he started it.

Building site/factory employee
When Shaun was interviewed for his job, his supervisor asked him if he could make tea. Shaun said, 'Yes'. 'And can you drive a fork lift truck?' his boss continued. 'Why?' asked Shaun, 'How big is the teapot?'

Bus driver/taxi driver
A woman asked Reg if he stopped/could stop at the Ritz. 'No, madam, not on my wages,' he replied.

Buyer/contracts officer/negotiator
Stephen would never accept a bribe. One day he was offered a Porsche. He was indignant, 'I cannot accept a gift like that,' he fumed. 'I quite understand,' replied the would-be briber, 'I tell you what, why don't I sell it to you for a fiver?' Stephen thought about it for a minute. 'In that case, I'll take two.'

Car dealer
Arthur pointed to an old Escort. 'I can't shift this,' he said, 'I'll have to reduce it.' 'By how much,' I asked. 'Oh, by about three owners and 50,000 miles,' he replied.

Chemist/pharmacist
Sign over pharmacy: 'We dispense with accuracy'.

Computer worker
Jill and her manager were examining the printout from the new computer in their department. Eventually Jill turned to her boss and remarked, 'Do you realise it would have taken 500 men 1000 years to make a mistake that big.'

Customs officer
Wayne asked a man whether he had any pornographic material. 'Pornographic material?' he replied, 'I haven't even got a pornograph.'

Dentist/doctor/vet
I arranged to meet Lee after work at his surgery. I was a bit early so I glanced through the magazines he provides for his patients in the waiting room. Wasn't it terrible about the *Titanic*?

DSS employee
Jimmy told me about a lady who asked if something could be done for her. 'I've got no clothes,' she said, 'and the vicar visits me three times a week.'

Farmer
Joe was having great trouble with hikers walking across his land. So he put up a notice on one of his gates: 'Trespassers admitted free. The bull will charge later.'

Firefighter
She told him to go to blazes so he became a fireman.

Grocer/butcher/etc.

Alf told me about the little old lady who makes the same order every Thursday: 'Three pounds of potatoes, please, and could you make them small because the big ones are so heavy to carry.'

Hairdresser/barber

A person who talks behind your back.

Hotel worker

Basil tells me that business is so bad that the Astoria is now stealing towels from its guests.

Insurance office employee

Muhammad says people write some very strange things on their insurance claim forms. Here are a couple he told me about: 'The man was all over the place on the road – I had to swerve several times before I hit him.' And here's another: 'I was thrown out of my car and was found in a ditch by some cows.'

Laundry/dry cleaner employee

A hundred years ago there were no laundries or dry cleaners. In those days people had to tear their own buttons off.

Librarian/book shop employee

A man asked Sarah, 'Have you a book entitled *"Man, Master of the Home"*?' She looked at him in disbelief for a moment and then replied, 'Try the Fiction department'.

Manager/director

A big gun who has managed not to get fired.

Newsagent

It's Aruna's second paper shop. The first one blew away.

Night-watchman/person on permanent night shifts/etc.

A man who earns his living without doing a day's work.

Nurse

At the dress rehearsal, when Dougal held out the ring, Florence took his pulse.

Police officer/traffic warden/AA/RAC/etc.
A motorist pulled up at the Coldra Junction and asked Jeremy whether it mattered whether he took the A48 or M4 to Cardiff. 'Not to me, it doesn't,' Jeremy replied.

Post office employee
Pat, isn't it odd that if a letter is too heavy, you have to put more stamps on it, not less?

Public house/brewery/off-licence employee
Jack loves his work at the 5-X Brewery. In fact he often takes his work home with him.

Railway employee
A man said he wanted to catch the late train to Manchester. 'Take the 11.15,' Casey suggested. 'That's usually as late as any.'

Salesperson
John is the most independent salesman I know. He doesn't take orders from anybody.

Shop-keeper
Have you seen the sign in Mark's shop window? It says: 'Don't go elsewhere to be cheated. Come in here'. And what about the sign inside? It says: 'Our boast is that we never allow a dissatisfied customer to leave this shop.'

Solicitor
A person who makes sure that you get what's coming to him.

Supermarket worker
A supermarket is a place where shoppers should put all their eggs in the same basket. Have you seen the new sign in Betta-Buys? What a bargain. It says 'Eggs still twelve to the dozen.'

Tax inspector/dentist/any other 'unpopular' occupation
There's a sign outside Jim's office, it says, 'Sorry – we're open.'

Teacher
Barry asked if anyone in his class could correct this sentence: 'It was me what done it.' A little lad at the back stood up and said, 'Sir, it was

not me what done it.' A few days later the lad struck again. He asked, 'Sir, can I be punished for something I haven't done?' 'Of course not,' Barry replied. 'That's good,' he said, 'because I haven't done my homework.'

Television repairs/any other repairs job

A rather aged gent went into Tariq's Repairs. 'I brought my TV in for repairs in 1978 but then the Old Bill paid me a visit and – well I only got out this morning,' he explained, handing Tariq a very crumpled old ticket. Tariq retreated to the back room and was gone for about twenty minutes. He returned and handed the ticket back to the old man, saying, 'We should have it ready for you by next Friday, sir.'

Union official

Jack takes his responsibilities very seriously. Last summer he sent me a postcard from Minorca. It said, 'Having a wonderful time and a half.'

Waiter/waitress

A customer called Bruce over and said, 'Waiter, this egg is bad.' 'It's not my fault, sir,' Bruce replied, 'I only laid the table.'

Window cleaner

George is a perfectionist. He told me that when he cleans the windows at the top of the Nelson Mandela high rise flats, he often feels like stepping back to admire his work.

HOBBIES

Amateur boxing/judo/karate

David is a very colourful fighter – black and blue usually.

Amateur dramatics

I remember the day Steve came home and told me he'd got his first part. 'I play a man who's been married for twenty-five years,' he announced. 'That's a great start, son,' I said, 'Just keep at it and one of these days you'll get a speaking part.'

Archaeology

I asked Max what an archaeologist was. He said it was a man whose whole life lies in ruins.

Book collecting

Nicholas is so proud of his book collection. Last week he complained to me that he now has so many that he just doesn't know what to do with them. I suggested that he tried reading them.

Card schools

Marcus used to really enjoy our Saturday night card schools. But I remember one evening when he jumped up from the table, white with rage. 'Stop the game!' he yelled, 'Steve's cheating!' 'How do you know?' I asked. 'Because he's not playing the hand I dealt him.'

Cars

Mike's car is his pride and joy. Last month it cost him £300 to have it overhauled. He was speeding down the M1 when a police car overhauled it.

Cats

Kim told me Arthur is a very sensible cat. He never cries over spilt milk.

CD/record collecting

Adam has a magnificent CD collection. One day he went into a record shop and asked for *Rhapsody in Blue* but the girl said they hadn't got it. 'Well would you mind taking another look?' he asked. 'Perhaps they do it in some other colour.'

Cinema/theatre/bingo

Harrison left in the middle of the film and trod on the foot of the woman at the end of the row. When he returned, he said, 'Did I tread on your foot on the way out?' 'Yes,' she replied. 'Good,' he said, 'then this is my row.'

Cooking

People are always asking Keith for his recipes. I suppose they're hoping he'll give away his only copy.

Dancing

As we skipped the light fandango, I told Sue that I had learnt to dance in just one evening. 'I thought so,' she said.

Dogs

Keith told me that his dog, Fido, is just like one of the family. I'm still trying to work out which one.

Fashion
As you know, Sally is really into fashion. She just told me the latest hot news and, Kevin, you'd be wise to take note of it. There will be absolutely no change in pockets this year.

Fishing
Peter says he loves going fishing because it gives him something to do while he's not doing anything.

Flying
I don't know how Orville can go up in those gliders. I get air sick when I lick an airmail stamp.

Football
Roy was on the bench and Rovers were getting hammered. The manager turned to him and said, 'Get in there and get frantic'. Roy jumped up and said, 'OK, boss. He's their striker, right?'

Gambling
Terry told me he dreamt he won a million on the pools/horses/national lottery. June said to him, 'What shall we do about all the begging letters?' 'Just keep sending them,' he replied.

Golf
Ahmin has been in more sand than Lawrence of Arabia. And when he lowers his head on the green, he's not just preparing to putt, he's praying.

Gymnastics
Roger tells me he works out for half an hour a day on the vaulting horse. Yesterday he fell off. But he's not blaming the horse because it was his vault.

Hiking/walking
Ian had hoped to climb Ben Nevis during his holiday, but he didn't get any farther than Fort William – it took him five days to walk there and two to refold the maps.

Hitch-hiking
Ford always begins his hitch-hiking at 3 in the morning. He said it's the best time to miss the traffic.

Holidays/travel
Last summer Martin went to Iceland and Texas. This year he's going to Sainsburys and MFI.

Jogging
Sally says the only reason she took up jogging was so she could hear heavy breathing again.

Karaoke
When Frank sings his head off, it really improves his appearance.

Motorbike trials/racing car trials/sheep dog trials/etc.
I went with Phil to the 199- Scottish sheep dog trials. 31 were found guilty.

Musician
Simon asked his music teacher for her honest opinion of his compositions. She looked him straight in the eye and said, 'I believe your songs will be played when Beethoven and the Beatles are forgotten – but not before.'

Photography
I'm not too sure what kind of photographs David takes, but I can tell you that he has to develop them in the dark.

Pony club/gymkhana/horse riding
Lucinda called her pony Radish and she used to tell everyone it was her horse Radish.

Pop group
Elton says they're going to change the name of their band to Free Beer. Great name, isn't it? Think of how it will look on pub notice boards. The punters will pile in.

Reading
Khadija asked the librarian if he could suggest a good book – something quite deep. He replied, 'How about *20,000 Leagues Under The Sea*?'

Skiing
Like Eddie, I thought of taking up skiing – but I let it slide.

Sport (any)
Bill asked the vicar if he'd be committing a sin if he played golf on the

Sabbath. He said the way he played it would be a sin on any day.

Stamp-collecting
Philately will get you everywhere.

Swimming
I asked Duncan where he learnt to swim. 'In water,' he replied dryly.

Tennis
André practises by hitting a tennis ball against his garage door. It's really improved his game. He hasn't won yet, but last week he took the door to five sets.

Water skiing
Adrian got a pair of water skis for Christmas. He spent the next six months looking for a lake on a slope.

WEDDING JOKES AND ONE-LINERS

Any of the quotations, jokes, stories and one-liners given so far can be adapted and personalised for any wedding speech. However, here are some lines which are likely to be particularly useful for each of the main speeches.

For the bride's father
Ladies and Gentlemen, it has been said that love is the light and sunshine of life. We cannot enjoy ourselves, or anything else, unless someone we love enjoys it with us. Well from this day forth Mavis and Derek will be enjoying their lives together . . . [Or some other appropriate quotation hook – see Chapter 2]

I hope you all enjoyed your warm beer and porky scratchings.

Nice to see you all dressed up in those dicky bows. Are you here for the snooker?

My function today is simple, to give away the bride. Of course, after paying for this lot, the bride is about all I have left to give away.

Today I gave away my daughter – and you will never believe the pleasure that gave me.

Ian said, 'I want your daughter for my wife.' 'Why?' I said, 'what would your wife do with her?'

I was so proud to see her today as she swept down the aisle. Proud and surprised – I'd never seen her sweep anything before.

I would like to say that Maggie's really excellent around the house . . . I really would like to say that . . . wish I could.

I'm sure you'll agree Lucy looks absolutely stunning today . . . and the nice thing is, she's as lovely on the inside as she is on the outside.

It's easy to meet expenses – everywhere you go there they are.

Always remember that money comes first and last. You've got to make it first and then make it last.

I asked my wife if she remembered our wedding night. 'Steve,' she said, 'that was 27 years ago, there's no need to apologise now.'

I shall never forget my marriage because I had to ask my wife's mother permission to marry her daughter. 'Have you the means to make her happy?' she asked. 'Well,' I said, 'it'll make her laugh and I'm afraid that's the best I can do.'

This morning my sin-in-law became my son-in-law.

I've come to think of Tim as I do my own son – the one I threw out and disowned.

I love the idea of becoming a grandfather – but I'll have to get used to being married to a grandmother.

Advice? When you feel a quarrel brewing up one of you should immediately leave the house. That's why I look so well – I get plenty of fresh air.

Let the bride know who's boss from the start. There's no point in trying to fool yourself.

Live each day as if it were your last, and each night as if it were your first.

Jayne is the best daughter any parents could have asked for. And if I'm accused of being biased, then I plead guilty – and proud of it.

Mary is the best daughter in the world – she is beautiful, charming, intelligent and, well, perfect in every way. She does everything for me – she even wrote this speech.

Try praising your wife, even if it does frighten her at first.

When Tony asked me for Cherie's hand in marriage, I asked, 'Tony, do you think you're earning enough to support a family?' 'Yes,' he replied. 'Think very carefully now,' I added, 'after all you know there are six of us.' Only joking Tony. But I do want you to know you really are one of the family now . . .

Hamish asked me if I thought he was old enough to marry Carrie. 'Oh yes,' I replied, 'because you'll age fast enough.'

When Henry Ford was asked his secret for a long and happy marriage, he replied, 'The formula I recommend is one I have always used in making cars – just stick to the same model.'

When we got married my wife didn't have a rag on her back. But she's got plenty of them now.

I read that marriage was going out of fashion. Well, if that's true, have you ever seen two people looking so happy to be out of fashion?

I can still hear my bride-to-be saying to her mother, 'Mum, I've still got so much to do and I want everything to be perfect. I'm determined not to overlook even the most insignificant detail.' And her mother replying, 'Don't worry, I'll make sure he's there.'

The best way not to forget your wife's birthday is to forget it once.

After we'd been married for about a month, one evening I asked, 'You don't mind if I point out a few of your faults, do you?' 'Not at all,' she replied, 'it's those little faults that stopped me from getting a better husband.'

Sometimes Liz is a little economical with the truth. But, to be fair to her, that's the only thing she's economical with.

Zoë admits that she does have some faults, but she insists that ever being wrong isn't one of them.

I could offer you lots of excellent advice. Advice that's been passed down from generation to generation and ignored by all of them. So instead I'll simply say . . .

On the sea of matrimony you have to expect occasional squalls.

I knew my wife-to-be could keep a secret because we had been engaged for weeks before even I knew anything about it.

Indira never loses her temper, but occasionally she mislays it.

Any man who thinks he is smarter than his wife is married to a very smart woman.

One day I found Liz playing with her new housekeeping set. 'Are you washing dishes?' I asked. 'Yes,' she replied, 'and I'm drying them too, because I'm not married yet.' Hugh, you have been warned.

The best way to avoid quarrels? Let her go her way, you go hers.

And a word of advice to you both: the best way to get the last word in any argument is to say 'sorry'.

If I were asked for a recipe for a long, happy marriage, I would say the formula lies in two simple words: 'Yes, dear'.

Advice to the bridegroom? Easy. When she hands you a dishcloth, blow your nose and hand it back.

Rodney and Cassandra first met in a revolving door and they've been going round together ever since.

As we were on our way to the wedding this morning, my wife turned to me and said, 'You know, you don't seem quite as well dressed as when we were married 25 years ago.' I replied, 'Well I don't know why not, I'm wearing the same suit.'

If a man tries as hard to keep his wife after marriage as he tried to get her, they will get along very well.

Ladies and Gentlemen, will you please stand, raise your glasses and drink a toast to the health and happiness of the bride and groom!

For the bridegroom

I'd like to thank Albert for his kind words. It's amazing what some people will say when they're not under oath.

This is the happiest day of my entire life, and I really must thank Suzy for pointing that out.

I really couldn't ask for a better woman. If I did, Sharon would kill me.

I would like to say a word of thanks to the bridesmaids. You did your job magnificently. Obviously I will use you every time I get married from now on.

Rhys is in a position to marry anyone he pleases. The problem is he doesn't seem to be able to please anyone.

Roger will be getting up to speak in a moment or two, and I can tell you he has some very unusual material, beginning with his suit.

I do not deserve the good things that have been said of me – but I will try to deserve them, and to be worthy of my wife.

Our thanks must go to our parents. Without them none of this would have been possible.

I can't imagine a happier way to start married life than with our family and friends around us.

I asked her father if I could marry her and he said, 'Just leave your name and phone number and we'll be in contact if nothing better comes up.'

Next I must thank Faruq for being best man, though I'm not sure how thankful to be because I haven't heard his speech yet.

I think Donny's suit looks terrific. I know he won't mind if I let you all into a little secret – he always wears it when he goes to our monthly football social evenings *[or whatever]*. As we left for the church this morning, little Jimmy grabbed him by the arm and asked why he was wearing it today when he knew it always gives him such a headache the next morning.

Thank you for your presence – both senses of the word.

They say marriage is a lottery. If it is, I have hit the jackpot.

Those of you who do not know Fred are the luckiest people in the world. That's because the pleasure of getting to know him lies ahead of you.

She told me we were not marrying for better or for worse, but for good.

They say a girl grows to be like her mother; well, I can only hope it is true.

These delightful/charming *[safer than beautiful]* young ladies have done a great job in helping Sarah up the aisle – although I hope she came to the church of her own free will.

I have one final duty – no, not duty, pleasure – and that is to propose a toast to the health of the bridesmaids. . .

Ladies and Gentlemen, the bridesmaids!

So the bridegroom's speech is really a general thank you speech. If anyone has made a special effort to attend your wedding – possibly travelling a long distance – you should thank them publicly. If their first language is not English, learn a little phrase in their native tongue. This will make a very good impression. If this isn't possible, at the very least learn how to say 'thank you'. Here is how 'thanks' are said around the world.

A world of thanks

Arabic: *Shoukran*
Chinese: *Doh shieh (doe she)*
Czech: *Dekuji*
Danish: *Takk*
Dutch: *Dank U wel*
Finnish: *Kiitos* (key-toss)
French: *Merci* (mare-see)
German: *Danke* (dan-care)
Greek: *Efharisto*

Hebrew: *Todah rabah* (toda raba)
Hindi: *Danyavad*
Hungarian: *Koszonom*
Indonesian: *Terima kasih* (terima kassee)
Italian: *Grazie* (grat-see)
Japanese: *Arigato*
Korean: *Komapsumnida*
Malay: *Terima kasih* (terima

kassee)
Norwegian: *Takk*
Polish: *Dziekuke* (duz-ee-kugee)
Portuguese: *Obrigo* (masc.);
   Obrigada (fem.)
Rumanian: *Multumiri*
Russian: *Spasiba*
Serbo-Croat: *Hvala* (huvala)

Spanish: *Gracias*
Swahili: *Asanti*
Swedish: *Takk*
Thai: *Khop khun* (chop cun)
Turkish: *Tesekkur*
Urdu: *Shukria*
Vietnamese: *Cam on ong*
Yiddish: *Dank*

If possible, confirm your pronunciation with a native speaker.

For the best man

Ladies and Gentlemen, this is truly an historic day! [Followed by an anniversary hook – see Chapter 2.]

Ladies and Gentlemen, as Henry VIII said to each of his wives in turn, 'I shall not keep you long'! [Or some other humour hook – see Chapter 2.]

It seems a little strange replying to the toast to the bridesmaids because, as you can see, I'm not a bridesmaid.

On behalf of the bridesmaids I would like to thank John for that toast. But to be honest I don't think he did them justice. Never mind – today who can blame him? Clearly he only has eyes for Janet. I'm still single and emotionally unblinkered and I think they are the most delightful set of bridesmaids I've ever seen.

My job today is to talk of Steven – and there are no skeletons in his cupboard – or so I thought . . .

Dear Fred, utterly unspoilt by failure.

It is impossible to praise this guy too highly . . . it's impossible to praise him at all.

Doesn't Dean look great? They made wonderful suits in the 'seventies.

This couple is bound to be happy because they're both so very much in love with the bridegroom.

If I ever needed a brain transplant, I'd choose Jim's because I'd want one that had never been used.

There is absolutely nothing wrong with Steve that a miracle can't fix.

Linda, I've got some good news and some bad news about Paul's boozing habits. Here's the good news: he's told me he's not drinking anymore. Here's the bad news: he's told me he's not drinking any less either.

Lee is a man of many parts – some still in working order.

They say blood is thicker than water. Nathan is thicker than both.

Jim is very responsible. If there's a problem, you can be sure he's responsible.

May your luck be like the capital of Ireland: always Dublin.

I'm supposed to sing the bridegroom's praises and tell you all about his good points. Unfortunately, I can't sing, and I can't think of any good points.

Alf, if Audrey doesn't treat you as she should – be thankful.

It only takes one drink to get Steve drunk – the fourteenth.

Joe is a very modest man – and he has plenty to be modest about.

Noel really has hidden talents. I just hope some day he'll find them.

Soon after we met, Dave invited me to his eighteenth birthday party and he gave me details of his address and how to get there. He said, 'A number 8 bus will bring you right to my door – 117 Alma Road. Walk up to the front door and press the doorbell with your elbow.' 'Why my elbow?' I asked. 'Because you'll have the wine in one hand and my pressie in the other, won't you?'

You may have noticed how few single people were invited to the wedding. I will let you into a secret: that was Ray's idea. He's very astute.

He told me that if he invited only married people all the presents would be clear profit.

There's nothing I wouldn't do for Ryan, and I know there's nothing he wouldn't do for me. In fact, we spend our lives doing nothing for each other.

I asked my wife how she would like to celebrate our wedding anniversary. 'How about with two minutes silence,' she replied.

A man like Alan only comes along once in a lifetime – I'm only sorry it had to be during *my* lifetime.

We've been happily married for two years and this year we celebrate our fifth anniversary.

This is a day to remember! The day John bought the drinks.

It was a beautiful ceremony. I found it very moving to witness Timothy taking his two marriage vows: Silence and Poverty.

I told my wife that we hadn't been able to agree on anything during our four years of marriage. 'Five years,' she replied.

I have already congratulated the groom. I said, 'Jason, you will always look back on this day as the happiest day of your life.' This was yesterday.

My neighbour blows his wife a kiss every morning as he leaves for work. Louise asked me why I don't do the same. I said, 'But I hardly know the woman.'

When Mark was asked about the arrangements for the wedding, he said, 'I'll leave all that to you, but we must have Bells – and at least a dozen bottles.'

There's no doubt about it, men have better taste than women. After all, Paul chose Christina – but Christina chose Paul.

Our beautiful bride has always said that she wanted a very simple wedding and that's what she got – starting with the groom.

This marriage will last a lifetime. And, as you know, that's unusual these days. I know a couple who broke up before their wedding pictures were developed. And they used one of those paranoid cameras.

May bad luck follow you all your life – and never catch up with you.

Gavin doesn't know the meaning of the word meanness. Mind you, he doesn't know the meaning of lots of other words either.

For the bride
My husband and I . . .

I'm very glad to break with tradition and say a few words of my own on this happy occasion.

My father knew that the most important thing he could do for his children was to love their mother.

And thank you for your wonderful wedding presents – with all those saucepans and toasters I only hope he likes boiled toast.

My mother told me that thirty years of marriage has taught her that the best way for a wife to have a few minutes to herself is to start doing the dishes.

He may think he's going to be boss in the house, when actually he's going to be housing the boss.

Mum told me the only time a woman really succeeds in changing a man is when he's a baby – so I still have time to change Simon.

This is my happiest day since I was in the arms of another woman's husband – my mother's.

And thanks to my own parents for taking care of me so well all my life and also for recognising that Javed was the right man to hand me over to.

Alan Jones, this is your wife!

GOOD LINES WHEN THINGS GO WRONG

Rod Stewart sang about 'well rehearsed ad-lib lines'. A good speech-maker must be able to think on his or her feet but here are a few lines you could use under the right circumstances:

A speech-maker isn't around when required
I think Wayne must be up on the roof. I suppose it's my fault really, I shouldn't have told him the drinks were on the house. We'd better send out a search-party . . .

Your microphone starts playing up
Well, Mike, that is the end of our double act; I'm going solo. *[Then speak without it.]*

You forget a name or get it wrong
I'm so sorry, there are three things I always forget: names, faces and, er . . . I can't remember the other.

A glass or bottle smashes
I'm pleased you're having such a smashing time.

A tray falls
No, please, save your applause until I've finished.

A vehicle with a siren passes nearby
Well I'd better wind up before they come to get me.

Someone arrives late
Please come in. Sit down there. I'm so glad you could make it *[don't embarrass them by saying it sarcastically]*. You've arrived just in time to toast Anne and Nick. I was just telling everyone how they met while they were working for . . .

A waiter keeps rushing around in front of you
I think he must have a train to catch.

Someone interrupts (good-natured)
Yes, Bill, I do remember that – how could I forget it? And I also remem-

ber something that happened a few months later [*then back to your speech*].

Someone continually interrupts (bad-natured)

[*A tricky situation because he or she is someone's guest. Try to be amusing.*] I suggest you lean against the wall – that's plastered too.

The weather is atrocious or too good

I shall keep this short, in case we get snowed in/swept away in the storm/before all the ice melts.

A catch-all when anything at all goes wrong

Jeremy, I hope that camcorder is still running. That is certain to be worth £250.

6
Coping with Nerves

It is perfectly natural and normal to feel a little nervous when delivering a speech. In fact, it helps if you do. The adrenalin will flow and you will be charged up and ready to give a really great performance.

However, if you feel too nervous the quality of your speech will suffer. The single best way to try and avoid this happening is to make sure you are properly prepared. If you know what ground you are going to cover (although not necessarily the exact words you are going to use), and you are well-rehearsed, this is bound to increase your confidence and thereby also reduce your nervousness.

But even the best-prepared speech maker can suffer from a sudden attack of the collywobbles. So here are a few tricks of the trade to help you cope with them (or at least conceal them), both before and during your speech.

BEFORE YOUR SPEECH

As you sit there remind yourself that your audience will be on your side. This is a happy day. They are not a jury. They are willing you to do well. And, quite frankly, they won't give a damn if you do fluff a line or two.

Tell yourself that you are going to make a great speech. They will love you. Positive thinking like this really works – and it boosts self-confidence.

Whatever you do, don't drink too much. Booze is like success; it is great until it goes to your head. A glass or two to lift your morale is fine. Any more than that and you will be certain to fail the speech makers' breathalyser test. So don't drink and drivel.

Even if you are still feeling nervous, remember that you will be the only person in the room who knows it – 90% of our nervousness is internal; only 10% displays itself to the outside world. Unless you tell them you are nervous they won't know. So never, never tell them.

If you feel the pressure beginning to get to you, try one or two of these emergency relaxation techniques. They can be used anywhere and any time without anyone, except you, knowing it.

EMERGENCY RELAXATION TECHNIQUES

Breathing to reduce tension

1. Sit comfortably with your arms at your sides and breathe in deeply through your nose.

2. Hunch up your shoulders as high as you can, clench your fists, push your toes hard into the floor, tense your body even harder than it is now – and then still harder.

3. Hold your breath for a few seconds.

4. As you exhale slowly through your nose, loosen your shoulders and let them drop, unclench your fists and let your heels return to the floor. Imagine that your shoulders are dropping down as far as your waist and that your feet are so light that they are sinking into the ground.

Sitting at a table

1. Pull in your stomach muscles tightly. Relax.

2. Clench your fists tightly. Relax.

3. Extend your fingers. Relax.

4. Grasp the seat of your chair. Relax.

5. Press your elbows tightly into the side of your body. Relax.

6. Push your feet into the floor. Relax.

Spot relaxation

1. Imagine that your shoulders are very heavy.

2. Hunch them up.

3. Drop them down very slowly.

4. Gently tip your head forward and feel the muscles pulling up through the middle of your shoulder blades.

5. Move your head gently backwards and feel the tension in the muscles down the front of your neck.

6. Bring your head back to an upright position and breathe very deeply for a few moments.

Stopping negative thoughts

1. Tell yourself: *Stop!*

2. Breathe in and hold your breath.

3. Exhale slowly, relaxing your shoulders and hands.

4. Pause. Breathe in slowly, relaxing your forehead and jaw.

5. Remain quiet and still for a few moments.

Head in the clouds

1. Stare at the ceiling and visualise floating clouds.

2. Imagine you are drifting towards them.

3. Release your tension and watch it float away with the clouds.

4. Gradually return from the clouds, feeling calm, cool and collected in your thoughts.

Draining tension away

Imagine you are transparent and filled with your favourite colour liquid. The temperature is perfect. Then drain the liquid from your body through your fingers and toes. Feel the tension draining away with the fluid.

The decanter

Sit comfortably and imagine that your body is a decanter. The bottom of the bottle is your pelvis and hips and the top is your head. As you breathe in, picture the air as pure energy gradually filling up the decanter. Hold the energy for a few seconds and then see it slowly pouring out as you exhale.

The hammock

Imagine you have been walking along a beach for hours. You are very tired. Suddenly you spot a hammock at the top of a steep sand dune. You begin to climb the dune, but you are now becoming exhausted. *Only ten more steps to go, now nine* . . . you can hardly stand up . . . *now eight, seven, six* . . . feel the agony of each step upwards . . . *four, three* . . . Not far now . . . *two, one*, you make it! Collapse into the hammock and relax completely.

The stairway

As you sit in your chair, pick a spot on the wall, slightly above your eye level, and stare at it. Do not allow your attention to waver. Take three long breaths, with normal breathing for about ten seconds between each of them. Each time you exhale think the word *relax*, and let every muscle and nerve in your body go loose and limp. After you have said *relax* for the third time, close your eyes. Imagine you are at the top of a stairway. At the bottom of the stairs is complete relaxation. Visualise yourself descending. With each step you will become more and more relaxed. *20*, deeper in relaxation; *19* deeper; *18* deeper; and so on down to *1*. At that point you will be completely relaxed.

Meditation of the bubble

Picture yourself sitting quietly and comfortably at the bottom of a clear lake. Every time you have a negative thought, imagine it inside a bubble which gently rises out of your vision towards the surface. Then calmly wait for your next thought. If it is negative, watch it slowly rise towards the surface in another bubble. If you prefer, visualise yourself sitting next to a campfire with all your negative words and images rising in puffs of smoke, or sitting on the bank of a river with all your tension, fears and anxieties inside logs which are gently floating away from you.

Your favourite place

Visualise your favourite place – real or imagined: past, present or future. This is your very own secret place; and because it is in your mind, no one else need ever know about it. Perhaps it is in a beautiful valley by a gently flowing stream; or perhaps it is in a spaceship travelling to Mars. It is entirely up to you. Use all your senses – *see* the blue sky, *hear* the gurgling stream, *smell* the scented flowers, *taste* the cool water, *touch* the warm grass. Really *be there*. This idea may sound silly, but it isn't, for one simple reason – it works. Remain at your favourite place until you feel perfectly relaxed and ready to return to face the real world.

DURING YOUR SPEECH

However nervous most people feel before making a speech, their nerves will almost certainly evaporate once they are introduced and they begin to speak. Think about it this way: most footballers feel nervous, especially before a big game. But once they hear the shrill of the first whistle, their nerves seem to disappear. The reason? At that moment all their pent up tension is released and they can finally get on with the job in hand.

But if you do still feel nervous, here are a few tips to help you cope:

- As you begin your speech, smile naturally, find a few friendly faces and maintain plenty of eye contact with them. As your confidence grows, look more and more at other people around the rest of the room.

- Never admit that you are the slightest bit nervous.

- If you begin to shake, concentrate on your knees. Try to shift the shaking down to your kneecaps. You will find that most of it will evaporate en route. Whatever does arrive there will be hidden behind the table.

- Keep your notes on the table so they can't rattle or end up all over the floor.

- Don't draw attention to your hands.

- Don't hold a hand-mike; leave it on its stand.

- Be aware of any possibly annoying personal habit you may have – such as twitching – and make a positive effort to control it.

- If your mouth becomes dry and your throat tightens up, the obvious thing to do is to take a sip of water. But if this isn't possible, imagine you are sucking an orange.

But the best way to keep your nerves in check is to know that you have prepared a really great little speech. And make sure it *is* a little speech. As the mother whale said to her young: 'Remember, my dears, you can be harpooned only when you're spouting.' So don't go spouting on and on. Stand up to be seen, speak up to be heard, and then shut up to be appreciated. Good luck!

7
Fifty Model Speeches

Finally, it's time to put it all together by taking a look at some model speeches.

You can use these in one of three ways. You could select the one that best suits you and then adapt and personalise it, or take what you think to be the best bits from two or more speeches and adapt and personalise them, or plan your own speech from scratch after reading these just for inspiration.

The usual order of speeches is:

1. Toast to the bride and groom (model speeches 1–21).
2. Response to toast to the bride and groom and toast to the bridesmaids (model speeches 22-40).
3. Response on behalf of the bridesmaids (model speeches 41-50).

Traditionally, the first speech is made by the bride's father; the second by the bridegroom; and the third by the best man. However, this pattern assumes that the bride has been brought up by two parents and today over two million people in Britain haven't been. So now it is perfectly acceptable for speeches to be made by other people – perhaps by a close relative or family friend, by the bride's mother, or by the bride herself. It all depends on the particular circumstances of the bride and groom.

A READYMADE SELECTION

For those of you who do not want to wade through all these model speeches, here is a summary of which of them best suit these particular personal circumstances.

One of the couple was brought up in a single-parent family: Model speeches 5, 6, 7, 18, 19, 20, 25, 26, 36 and 37.

One of their parents is recently deceased: Model speeches 3, 4, 16, 17, 23, 24, 34 and 35.

They already have a child: Model speeches 11, 12, 13, 30, 31 and 32.

There were no bridesmaids at the wedding: Model speeches 21, 39, 40, 47 and 48.

It is a second marriage: Model speeches 8, 9, 10, 27, 28 and 29.

Nobody should ever be forced to speak, if they do not want to. This is supposed to be a happy day, so no-one should be forced to do anything. However, if anyone is going to speak, they should know about it well in advance, and they must know the precise *purpose* of their speech. Is it to propose a toast, to respond to a toast, or to do both?

The speeches should begin after the guests have finished eating. Make sure their glasses are charged *before* anyone speaks. If there is a toastmaster, he will say something like: 'Ladies and Gentlemen, pray silence for Mr Ben Nevis who will propose a toast to Mr Sydney and Mrs Pearl Harbour.' If there is no toastmaster, the best man should do the honours, possibly in a less formal manner: 'Ladies and Gentlemen, please be silent as Mr Ben Nevis proposes a toast to Mr Sydney and Mrs Pearl Harbour.'

Right, now let's take a look at 50 model speeches which, when adapted, personalised and possibly combined, should suit any particular set of circumstances.

TOAST TO THE BRIDE AND GROOM

At a formal wedding reception this opening speech should include some positive comments about the couple and some optimistic thoughts about love and marriage. At a more informal wedding party, the speech can be more general. At either setting it must all build up to the toast.

A good speech includes the right balance of humour and seriousness, all applied with liberal helpings of sentiment. But what is the right balance? That depends on the personalities of the couple and their backgrounds and circumstances. For example, a very humorous speech would be out of place if one of their parents died last month. It also depends on *your* personality. Do you feel comfortable telling a joke. If you don't, don't do it.

Model speech 1: Bride's father

Formal reception

Reverend Green, Ladies and Gentlemen – Friends, 'We cannot fully enjoy life unless someone we love enjoys it with us.' Not my words, I'm afraid, although how I agree with them.

I cannot begin to tell you how delighted I am to see my daughter, Karen, looking so radiant as she begins a new chapter of her life – as the wife and partner of Richard. I know I am also speaking for Mary when I say we are not losing Karen; we are merely entrusting her into Richard's care. And as we have got to know Richard well over the last few months, we have come to the inescapable conclusion that this will be very, very good care. He has shown himself to be exactly the sort of person we had always hoped Karen would marry: a man who knows where he's going in life – and how he's going to get there.

It seems like only yesterday that I found Karen playing with her new housekeeping set. 'Are you washing dishes?' I asked. 'Yes,' she replied, 'and I'm drying them as well because I'm not married yet.' Richard, you have been warned.

Looking around me, I see a picture of sartorial elegance. You'd put the Royal Ascot crowd to shame. But my wife isn't quite so sure about my appearance. As we were on our way to the wedding this morning, Mary turned to me and said, 'You know, you don't seem quite as well dressed as when we were married 25 years ago.' 'Well I don't know why not,' I replied, 'because I'm wearing the same suit.'

It is customary on an occasion such as this for the father of the bride to pass on a few words of wisdom about the institution of marriage. Well if 25 years of blissful marriage have taught me anything – and I pass this advice on to both of you – it is that the best way to get the last word in any argument is to say 'sorry'. But better still, of course, why argue in the first place?

Everyone who knows Karen and Richard believes that this has been one of those marriages made in heaven, and I know you will all want to join me in wishing them a long and happy married life together. So please stand up, raise your glasses and drink to the health and happiness of Karen and Richard.

To Karen and Richard!

Model speech 2: Close family friend, relative or godfather

Formal reception – where the bride's father is present but does not make a speech.

Ladies and Gentlemen, Anne's father, Phil, and her mother, Liz, have done me the great honour of offering me the opportunity of making this little speech on this joyous occasion, and to propose a toast to the happy couple. When I asked why they chose me, Phil explained that it was because we have been friends for more years than he cares to remember and that I have known Anne for all her life. Not so, Phil, I missed the first 24 hours.

You know, this is truly a historic day! This day, 13th July, will always be remembered because of three world-famous events. Film actor Harrison Ford was born in 1942; Live Aid pop concerts raised millions for charity in 1985; and on this day in 199-, Tim married Anne!

It seems like only yesterday since Anne's weekends were taken up with tap dancing, ballet and the pony club. She called her pony Radish and used to go round telling everyone it was her horse Radish.

But seriously, we're all very proud of the wonderful work she does for sick animals. And it was while she was helping out down at the RSPCA that she first met Tim.

Over the last few months I've got to know Tim well and I've come to the conclusion that he is a very pleasant, hard-working man with immaculate tastes. After all, he supports United and he chose Anne, didn't he?

Friends, I am sure that this young couple will have a wonderful marriage and I would ask you to join me now in wishing them a long, happy and prosperous future together. Please stand and raise your glasses. I propose a toast to the health and happiness of Anne and Tim.

To Anne and Tim!

Model speech 3: Close family friend, relative or godfather

Formal reception – where the bride's father is recently deceased.

Ladies and Gentlemen, it is a great honour for me to be here with you all today on this joyous occasion. I have known Clare and her parents for many years. It was 1980 when Henry, Sarah and a very young Clare became my next-door neighbours. Henry was an excellent gardener and he soon transformed not only his garden – but mine as well.

In fact we were in my greenhouse when he told me that Clare had met Francis. He spoke very highly of the young man on that June evening and on many subsequent occasions. Although we all greatly miss Henry, we can rejoice in the fact that he would have been absolutely delighted that Francis and Clare have become man and wife. And because his hopes and wishes have now been realised I feel that in a sense he is celebrating here with us today.

As you know, the wedding was postponed, but Clare is a girl well worth waiting for. Doesn't she look radiant? Henry would have been proud of her – as I'm sure Francis is. I have got to know Francis very well since we first met last summer and I know Clare has made a very wise choice. He is a hard-working lad who knows where he's going in life and how he's going to get there. These young people have a very bright future ahead of them and I would like you all to join me in wishing them every success as they begin their married life together. So please raise your glasses and drink to the health and happiness of Clare and Francis.

To Clare and Francis!

Model speech 4: Bride's father

Formal reception – where one of the bridegroom's parents is recently deceased.

Ladies and Gentlemen, it's been quite a week. England beat Holland, I won a few quid on the National and now, to crown it all, Ted married Carol. You know, I read in a newspaper the other day that marriage is going out of fashion. Well, you can't believe everything you read in newspapers. And even if it's true, have you ever seen two people so delighted to be out of fashion?

It seems only like yesterday since Carol's music was blasting through our household. I asked if I could borrow her CD for the evening. 'Do you fancy some heavy metal?' she asked. 'No just a bit of peace and quiet,' I replied. Come to think about it, it *was* yesterday.

But 'if music be the food of love, play on' because that's how Carol got to meet Ted. At a gig – I think that's what you call it – at the NEC. From there things just went from strength to strength. Over the last year or so I've got to know Ted well and I like to think we've grown into good friends. He's shown himself to be a very dependable young man and we've all been immensely impressed by the additional support he's given his mum since her sad loss. I only met Arthur twice, but that was enough to convince me that he was as happy at the prospects of his son's marriage as I was at my daughter's. So we can rejoice today that Arthur's hopes and wishes for his son have been realised.

It is customary for the bride's father to offer the newlyweds some profound piece of advice – advice that's been passed down from generation to generation and no doubt ignored by all of them. So instead I'll simply say to you both: Have a good life. I mean that. Ladies and Gentlemen, please stand, raise your glasses, and drink with me a toast to the health and happiness of Ted and Carol.

Ted and Carol!

(Where both the bride and bridegroom have recently lost a parent adapt and personalise the relevant parts of speeches 3 and 4.)

Model speech 5: Bride's mother
Formal reception – where the bride was brought up in a single-parent family.

Reverend Goodman, Ladies and Gentlemen, Dora just asked me, 'Would you like to speak now or should we let our guests enjoy themselves a little longer?' She always has had a way with words.

What a joy it is to see so many happy faces here today – and none happier than those of this young couple. And why not? Bryan has married Dora and Dora is gaining Bryan and losing me.

I was so proud to see Dora today as she swept down the aisle. Proud and surprised – I'd never seen her sweep anything before. But seriously, no one could have asked for more from a daughter. She deserves happiness and with Bryan I am confident she has found it.

Bryan is a very hard-working lad and we are all very proud of his recent success at City and Guilds. When he asked me for Dora's hand, I asked, 'Bryan, do you think you're earning enough to support a family?' 'Yes,' he replied. 'Think very carefully now,' I added, 'after all, you know there are five of us.' Only joking, Bryan. But I do want you to know you really are one of the family now.

Of course from time to time there will be problems, but I cannot imagine two people better equipped to face them. So I ask you all to be upstanding, to raise your glasses and to drink to the health and happiness of Dora and Bryan.

To Dora and Bryan!

Model speech 6: Close family friend, relative or godfather

Formal reception – where the bride was brought up in a single-parent family and her mother (or father) does not want to speak.

Ladies and Gentlemen, I am very honoured that Kylie's mother/father, Pat, asked me to propose a toast to the happy couple. I have known Kylie for many years and I have spent several pleasurable evenings watching her acting with the Plymouth Players. Well today there is no doubt that she is the star of the show – well, co-star anyway, alongside Jason.

I've got to know Jason well over the last few months and he has proved himself to be a very dependable, friendly and hard-working young man. Not only does he have a good job, but he is wisely continuing his education at night school. So, all being well, he should become a fully qualified chartered accountant within three years.

I am confident that Kylie and Jason have all the qualities needed to build a strong and successful marriage. They both have the sense of humour, love and support for one another necessary to help them through any difficult times, and the courage and determination to make sure things soon go right again. So let us raise our glasses and drink to the health and happiness of Kylie and Jason.

To Kylie and Jason!

Model speech 7: Bride's father

Formal reception – where the bridegroom was brought up in a single-parent family.

Ladies and Gentlemen, what an historic day this is! This very day, 1st June, will always be associated with three world-famous events. Screen legend Marilyn Monroe was born in 1926, The Beatles released the classic *Sergeant Pepper's Lonely Hearts' Club Band* in 1967, and on this day in 199-, Andrew married Myfanwy!

Thank you all so much for coming to celebrate this happy day. What a joy it is to see so many happy faces, and none more radiant than those of the young people on my right. Marriage, they say, is made in heaven. Well I'm afraid I beg to disagree. This marriage was not made in heaven, it was made at my retirement party when I introduced Andy to Myfanwy. I hasten to add that it was early retirement. Later that evening I remember my wife, Jean, commenting that they seemed to be getting on rather well. To be honest, I didn't take much notice at the time but four months later, when Andy asked my advice on engagement rings, I knew she was right.

And from that moment Myfanwy hardly stopped planning and arranging things to make sure everything went as smoothly as it did today. Even yesterday I overheard her say to her mother, 'Mum, I've still got so much to do and I want everything to be perfect. I'm determined not to overlook even the most insignificant detail.' And her mother replying, 'Don't worry, I'll make sure your father is there.'

Myfanwy is the best daughter any parents could have asked for. And if I'm accused of being biased, then I plead guilty – and proud of it. But everyone has faults – even Myfanwy. Andy, occasionally she is a little economical with the truth – but that is all she is economical with. For example, she certainly hasn't been economical with all the love and kindness she has displayed to her parents.

I worked with Andy for three years so I know him well. Our boss called him a miracle worker because it was a miracle if he worked. No, it's because I know Andy so well that I know I can get away with a crack like that. He has a great sense of humour and he really is a very hardworking young man. I know I'm not breaking any confidences when I tell you how proud his mother, June, is that he has decided to enrol for an Open University degree course.

As tradition demands, I shall pass on to you both one pearl of wisdom about the institution of marriage – it is the kind of advice you might expect from a former financial adviser: Marriage is an investment that pays dividends so long as you take the time to pay interest – and that's more than mere speculation.

I know, and you know, that these young people are going to be blissfully happy. Let us stand up, and raise our glasses and drink a toast to the health and happiness of Andy and Myfanwy.

To Andy and Myfanwy!

(Where both the bride and bridegroom were brought up in single-parent families adapt and personalise the relevant parts of speeches 6 and 7.)

We now must consider the thorny subject of speeches at second (and subsequent) weddings. Some people believe it best to make absolutely no reference to previous marriages. However, this tactic can backfire – especially if any of their children are present. For this reason others prefer to stop any gossipers in their tracks by being quite open about this aspect of their pasts. Why not ask the couple how they would like you to play it? If they want you to take the second approach, model speeches 8 to 10 should help.

Model speech 8: Bride's father
Formal reception or informal wedding party – where the bride has been married before.

Richard, for you this is a first marriage and a time of hope and excitement. For Elizabeth it is a second marriage. You are truly honoured. Despite all the difficulties of her first marriage, she decided she simply had to try again. You must have had some effect on her. This is a new start and, if you will forgive the cliché, today really is the first day of the rest of your lives. We all wish you everything that you wish yourselves and I would now like to propose a toast to your health and happiness.

To Richard and Elizabeth!

Model speech 9: Bride's father
Formal reception or informal wedding party – where the bridegroom has been married before.

Anne, for you this is a first marriage and a time of hope and anticipation. For Henry it is a second marriage. When he met you he decided that he simply had to marry again despite the difficulties of his first attempt. Anne, you must have had some effect on him. And think of it this way: the man you are marrying has already had the sharp corners rubbed off and he is already house-trained, so you won't have to bother with sandpaper or a litter tray.

But seriously, we sincerely hope you will always enjoy life together. This is a new start and, as they say, it is the first day of the rest of your lives. So let's raise our glasses and drink a toast to the health and happiness of Anne and Henry.

To Anne and Henry!

Model speech 10: Bride's father, close family friend or relative

Formal reception or informal wedding party – where both parties have been divorced or widowed at least once.

(Obviously, you will need to word your speech carefully, according to whether the parties have been widowed and/or divorced, and how long ago this happened.)

Ladies and Gentlemen, all marriages are special occasions but a second marriage is an unsurpassable event because no one goes into it looking through rose-tinted glasses. You know what kind of problems must be faced and what sort of mistakes must be avoided. And, of course, it is impossible to avoid such pitfalls until you first know they are there.

It cannot be easy later in life to put away the past and begin again but we know you have all the qualities needed to make this new chapter of your lives a great success. Everyone has the right to happiness – the grandmother as much as the granddaughter.

So we are all delighted that your times of loneliness and sadness are behind you. This is another chance to find true happiness; a time of renewed hope. And it is an honour for us to be here to share this new beginning with you. We are confident that you will now receive all the joy you so richly deserve. I know I speak for everyone present when I say we wish you all the very best for a wonderful future together. Ladies and Gentlemen, please join me in a toast to the health and happiness of Joan and Peter.

To Joan and Peter!

While we are considering potentially tricky situations, we must think about the kind of things you should say where the couple already has at least one child. Once again, it's best to ask them first, but a short, light, slightly humorous speech is safest.

Model speech 11: Bride's father

Formal reception or informal wedding party – where the couple already has at least one child.

Ladies and Gentlemen, marriage is an institution – but who wants to live in an institution? Well, here are two young people who have decided that their lives will be even happier in this institution – and we are delighted that they have.

For most people marriage is a bit of a lottery. Sometimes they find that the person they have married doesn't seem to be the same person they were engaged to. Bob and Paula don't need to worry about this. They know each other so well by now that they are certain their marriage will be a success. In many ways they have been far more sensible than the majority of us in finding this out before they tied the knot.

A successful marriage involves falling in love many, many times – but each time with the same person. We know Bob and Paula will continue to do this and will make sure that little Jodie is brought up in a strong, loving family unit – which is exactly how it should be. I was going to wish you both the best of luck for the future, but you have already proved that you don't need luck. So instead I will invite everyone to join me in a toast. Ladies and Gentlemen, let us drink to the health and happiness of Bob and Paula.

To Bob and Paula!

But perhaps only one of the couple is already a parent. Ask them if they want you to be open about this in your speech. If they do, you could say something similar to model speech 12.

Model speech 12: Bride's father
Formal reception or informal wedding party – where the bridegroom already has at least one child.

Ladies and Gentlemen, this is an historic day! This day, 14th March, will always be associated with three truly momentous events. The Russian Revolution ended in 1917; Michael Caine was born in 1933 (not a lot of people know that); and on this day in 199-, Mike married Sarah!

You know, it seems just like yesterday when I came home and found little Sarah grooming the dog. 'Don't worry,' she said, 'I'll put your toothbrush back in the bathroom afterwards, like I always do.' Well, from today she won't need my toothbrush because now she's got her very own groom.

During the time I've known Mike, I like to think we've become friends. At the same time Martha and I have also become great friends with his parents, Tom and Barbara. Then, of course, there is little Wendy. And who could not fall for her? But you know you can't fool kids. They are true judges of character and they tell it like it is. So I am absolutely delighted that Wendy loves Sarah as much as Sarah so clearly loves her.

I am reminded of a quotation by Bertrand Russell – reminded, that is, by Martha who looked it up last night: 'Of all forms of caution, caution in love is perhaps the most fatal to true happiness.' I am delighted that Sarah and Mike have thrown caution to the wind. Mike is a man who knows where he is going in life and I am confident he is the right man for Sarah. So can I ask you all to stand, raise your glasses, and drink a toast with me to the health and happiness of Sarah and Mike.

To Sarah and Mike!

Model speech 13: Bride's father
Formal reception or informal wedding party – where the bride already has at least one child.

Ladies and Gentlemen, 'Some talk of Alexander, and some of Hercules, and Hector and Lysander and such great names as these.' But I would rather talk about Sergeant and Mrs Wilson – about Terry and June.

June has been the best daughter any parents could have asked for – she is beautiful, charming, intelligent and, well, perfect in every way. She does everything for me – she even wrote this speech. Terry, June does admit to having one or two small faults but she insists that ever being wrong isn't one of them. And you certainly weren't wrong in choosing her.

I've known Terry for over two years now and he has proved himself to be a reliable, hard-working young man. And he gets on brilliantly with young David. You know you can't fool kids. They are true judges of character. And if they don't like you they won't pretend they do. Well, David does like Terry – very much indeed. And I know the feeling is reciprocal.

Bob Hope once said, 'Marriage is an institution and no family should be without one.' How I agree. Quite simply, Terry and June make a perfect match. So I ask you all to join me in drinking a toast to their health and happiness.

To Terry and June!

Model speech 14: Bride's father
Informal wedding party.

Ladies and Gentlemen, thank you for coming to celebrate this happiest of days. I would like to propose a toast to the happy couple, Pamella and Billy. May they enjoy good fortune, continued good health and immense happiness in their future together. May problems follow them all their lives – and never catch up with them.

To Pamella and Billy!

Model speech 15: A close family friend, relative or godfather

Informal wedding party – where the bride's father is present but does not make a speech.

Friends, I am honoured to have been asked to say a few words on this happy occasion. We all know that Judy and Richard are such fun-loving people [*or talented, lively, warm-hearted, generous, or clever people*] and that they are certain to bring the best out in one another. We wish them a long and happy marriage together and I ask you now to raise your glasses and drink to Judy and Richard.

To Judy and Richard!

Model speech 16: A close family friend, relative or godfather

Informal wedding party – where the bride's father is recently deceased.

Friends, it gives me special pleasure to be present at the wedding of my good friends Alf and Else. This is a lovely, small, intimate gathering of friends, which is just the way the happy couple wanted it. We all have personal knowledge of Alf's loyal friendship and kindness and we are delighted that he has married Else who is equally admired and respected for her qualities of generosity and warm-heartedness. How proud Arthur would have been of her today. Doesn't she look wonderful? I know how much Arthur was looking forward to this day so I feel we can all rejoice that his wishes for his daughter's happiness have now come true. So will you join me in drinking a toast to Alf and Else?

To Alf and Else!

Model speech 17: Bride's father

Informal wedding party – where one of the bridegroom's parents is recently deceased.

Ladies and Gentlemen, thank you all so much for joining my daughter, Alice and my new son, Danny, as they celebrate their first day of married life together. Few words are necessary because you know them both so well. You know what a determined young lady Alice is and how proud Rosemary and I are of her recent promotion. And you know what a charming, humorous and hard-working young man Danny is and how proud his dad, Frank, was of him. In a sense I feel he is celebrating here with his wife, Betty, because, like me, Frank believed they were made for each other. So let's raise our glasses and drink to Alice and Danny.

To Alice and Danny!

(Where both the bride and bridegroom have recently lost a parent adapt and personalise the relevant parts of speeches 16 and 17).

Model speech 18: Bride's mother
Informal wedding party – where the bride was brought up in a single-parent family.

Ladies and Gentlemen – Friends, I would like to propose a toast to the best daughter in the world and to the man who has been her husband for [*look at your watch*], for $58^1/2$ minutes – precisely. I am confident that they have a bright future together. I am not losing a daughter, I am gaining a son. So I ask you all to raise your glasses and to drink to their health and happiness.

To Susan and George!

Model speech 19: A close family friend, relative or godfather
Informal wedding party – where the bride was brought up in a single-parent family and her mother (or father) does not want to speak.

I am very honoured that Mary has asked me to propose a toast to the happy couple. We all know Wilma and Fred as fun-loving people [*or clever, generous, warm-hearted people*] who are sure to bring the best out in one another. They deserve the very best, so let's wish them a long and happy married life together.

Has everyone got a drink? Good. To Wilma and Fred!

Model speech 20: Bride's father
Informal wedding party – where the bridegroom was brought up in a single-parent family.

Friends, today has been a very happy day for all of us, and nobody in this room looks happier than the young couple sitting there. Obviously I know Esther very well and I can tell you, Desmond, you have made a very wise choice. Over the last year or so I've also got to know Desmond and his delightful mother, Rebecca, and I can tell you, Esther, you've made an equally wise choice. You were both made for each other.

Have you all got a drink? Good. Let's drink a toast to Esther and Desmond. To Esther and Desmond!

(Where both the bride and bridegroom were brought up in single-parent families adapt and personalise the relevant parts of speeches 19 and 20.)

Model speech 21: Best man
Informal wedding party with no bridesmaids.

I am very honoured, as I'm sure you are, to be here among this select little gathering today. We are all close friends or relatives of the happy couple, which is exactly how Tom and Jenny wanted it. Few words are necessary because you all already know of Jenny's unique qualities of kindness, loyalty and friendship. And we all admire the way Tom has worked so hard to get his new business off the ground. We wish him well. So all I will say is that I know I speak for you all when I say we are absolutely delighted that they have decided to tie the knot. Quite simply, they were meant for each other. So let's raise our glasses and drink to their health and happiness.

To Tom and Jenny!

RESPONSE TO THE TOAST TO THE BRIDE AND GROOM AND TOAST TO THE BRIDESMAIDS

The bridegroom responds to the toast to the bride and bridegroom making it clear he is speaking on behalf of both of them (unless his bride is going to speak as well – see speech 38). You must convey that you are conscious of the meaning of the occasion and its importance to you. It is really a general thank you speech. You thank the previous speaker for his or her kind words, your parents and your wife's for being such wonderful parents, the gathering for their good wishes and gifts, and all those who have helped to make the wedding ceremony and reception such successes. You then say some nice things about the bridesmaids before proposing a toast to them. If there are no bridesmaids and no maid/matron of honour, the toast is to your parents-in-law (see speech 40).

The speech should be very sentimental and should include the right balance of humour and seriousness. There is no hard and fast rule about what this balance should be. It really comes down to common sense. For example, if the bride or bridegroom was brought up in a single-parent family, it would be inappropriate to talk at any length about the sanctity of the institution of marriage. So, to a large extent, the content of your speech should reflect and be in tone with your background and personal circumstances, and with those of your wife.

Model speech 22: Bridegroom's reply
Formal reception.

Reverend Green, Ladies and Gentlemen, we are told that marriage is a lottery. Well if it is, then I have hit the jackpot. Quite simply, I am the luckiest man in the world to have a wife like Karen and to have friends like you to join us on this our happiest day. Happiest day so far that is because in the words of Karen's favourite Carpenters' song, 'We've only just begun. So much of life ahead. A kiss for luck [*blow her a kiss*] and we're on our way.' Yes Karen, we've only just begun.

But I've been lucky in so many other ways as well. Lucky in having the best parents in the world. Parents who knew that the most important thing they could do for their children was to love each other. Lucky in my new parents-in-law. What a horrible expression that is – parents-in-law. Let's call them parents-by-marriage. I'd like to thank them for giving us such a lovely wedding and reception, and, even more, for producing a daughter like Karen. And no one could have been luckier in their choice of best man. Doesn't he look terrific? I know he won't mind if I let you into a little secret – Alec always wears that suit when he goes to our monthly rugby social evenings. As we left for church this morning his five-year-old son, Christian, grabbed him by the sleeve and asked why he was wearing it today when he knew it always gave him such a headache the next morning.

But let's face it, Karen is a very lucky lady too. No, I don't mean because she married me, although I suppose she could have done worse. No, I mean because today she too has gained two wonderful parents-by-marriage. And she is lucky in the support she has received from her charming bridesmaids. I know how helpful to Karen they have been, not only today but in those long weeks of preparation that brides go in for. So before I sit down I ask you to join me in showing your gratitude to Tracy, Sharon and Dorien by offering them a toast.

Ladies and Gentlemen, the bridesmaids!

Model speech 23: Bridegroom's reply

Formal reception – where the bride's father is recently deceased.

Ladies and Gentlemen, my wife and I [*pause for laughter and applause*] would like to thank you all for your presence – in both senses of the word. I cannot imagine a happier way to start married life than with our friends and family around us, but you really have been ridiculously over-generous with your gifts.

I have a few personal thank yous to make too. George, I do not deserve the good things you have said of me – but I will try to deserve them, and to be worthy of my wife. Oh, how proud Henry would have been of Clare today. Doesn't she look wonderful? Thank you, Victoria, for allowing me to marry your beautiful daughter and for arranging this magnificent reception. And thanks also to my own parents. Both Clare and I have been very fortunate having grown up knowing the real meaning of marriage through the example of our parents.

Then of course I must thank James for being best man, though I'm not sure how thankful to be because I haven't heard his speech yet. And a special word of thanks is due to Hans and Gretel, my dear friends who have travelled all the way from Holland to be with us today. Hans, I've got a couple of bottles of schnapps in. Thank you both so much for coming – *dank U wel*.

Finally, what can I say about the bridesmaids, the charming young ladies who did such a great job in helping Clare up the aisle – although I hope she came to the church of her own free will. They have been wonderful and have added so much to the occasion, so please join me in drinking a toast to Victoria, Petunia, Primrose, and Zinnia.

Ladies and Gentlemen, the bridesmaids!

Model speech 24: Bridegroom's reply

Formal reception – where one of his parents is recently deceased.

Ladies and Gentlemen, thank you all so much for coming to our wedding and for being so generous with all your gifts. Carol will certainly find the lawn mower and electric drill useful and I will make full use of the deck chairs and the portable TV. Only joking, Carol. I'd like to take this opportunity to make a few personal thank yous too. Martin, thank you for those kind words – but why didn't you give me your tip for the National? *[This reference to the National shows the bridegroom was listening to the first speaker – and responding to what he said – because it was not in his draft speech.]* And thank you and Gail for producing a daughter such as Carol, and for laying on this wonderful reception. Thanks too to my mother simply for being my mother. Mum, Dad loved Carol almost as much as I do – *almost* as much. And how I agree with Martin that we can rejoice in the fact that the marriage he so much wanted has now taken place. *[Another unrehearsed response to the earlier speech.]* In a sense, I feel he is celebrating with us.

A special word of thanks is due to our attendants. My best man, Carl, is a man of hidden talents. I just hope that one day he'll find them. No, thanks Carl, you did a great job today. And so did these charming young bridesmaids. Don't they look a picture? Ladies and Gentlemen, will you please join me in drinking a toast to the bridesmaids?

The bridesmaids!

(Where both the bride and groom have recently lost a parent adapt and personalise the relevant parts of speeches 23 and 24.)

Model speech 25: Bridegroom's reply
Formal reception – where the bride was brought up in a single-parent family.

Reverend Goodman, Ladies and Gentlemen, thanks for those kind words, Mum. My wife and I *[pause]*, oh how I've waited to say those words. My wife and I are delighted that you were able to come to our wedding. I can't imagine a happier way to start married life than with our families and friends around us. And thank you all so much for your gifts. With all these saucepans and toasters it looks like I'm going to have to get used to boiled toast. But seriously, we do sincerely thank you for the wonderful gifts you have given us.

I have a couple of personal thank yous to make, too. I am especially grateful to Mary, my new mother-in-law, for helping arrange this reception and even more for bringing up Dora so well that she has become the lady you see before you today. And, of course, thanks to my parents for their contribution to today's festivities and for teaching me the difference between right and wrong, so I know which I'm enjoying at any particular time. Thanks must also go to Ian, my best man, who got me to the church on time.

I am also delighted that Auntie Hilda and Uncle Horace managed to make the long journey from Glasgow to be with us here today. Did you take the high road or the low road? Finally my sincere thanks go to the bridesmaids. They were wonderful and so well behaved. I know you will want to join me drinking a toast to the delightful young ladies who supported Dora so well on her big day.

Ladies and Gentlemen, the bridesmaids!

Model speech 26: Bridegroom's reply
Formal reception – where he was brought up in a single-parent family.

Ladies and Gentlemen, my wife and I *[pause]* are so pleased you are here to share what is the happiest day of our lives – so far. Thank you so much for your wonderful gifts – they really are exactly what we needed. I hope to get round to thanking you all personally later.

But first I would like to say a few other thank yous. First and foremost to Flo: thank you for marrying me. And thanks to her parents for making me feel like one of the family – and, of course, for arranging this wonderful gathering. Thanks, too, to my mother. In the fullness of time, if I am half as good at being one parent as my mother has been at being two, I will have succeeded beyond my wildest expectations.

And doesn't Radha look a picture – a real dandy. But I'll let you into a secret: he borrowed that suit from me. To be fair, he had ordered one but the trousers had to be altered. Yesterday they told him they wouldn't be ready in time. So he's going to sue them for promise of breeches. Now it is my duty – no, my pleasure to propose a toast to the bridesmaids. They all did their jobs magnificently. Please stand, raise your glasses, and drink a toast to the bridesmaids.

The bridesmaids!

(Where both the bride and bridegroom were brought up in single-parent families adapt and personalise the relevant parts of speeches 25 and 26.)

We must now consider the situations where the bridegroom and/or the bride have been married before. Some people decide to make no reference to this whatsoever, while others are quite open about it. It is entirely up to you. However, if you decide to take the first option, make sure that the person who proposes the opening toast, and your best man, are not going to say anything about it either. On the other hand, if you choose the second option, speeches 27 to 29 should help.

Model speech 27: Bridegroom's reply

Formal reception or informal wedding party – where the bride has been married before.

Ladies and Gentlemen – Friends, I would like to say a few sincere thank yous. First, thank you all for coming to our wedding, for your good wishes and for your most generous gifts. And of course thank you, Elizabeth, for taking me on. I promise that for you this will be second time lucky. We are not marrying for better or worse, we are marrying for good. Thanks also to Charles for those wise words. Yes, I am honoured. [*This was said in response to the first speaker – it was not in the draft speech.*] And thanks to you and Camilla for accepting me so readily into your family and also for laying on this wonderful reception/party. Then how could I forget my parents? Thanks Mam and Dad for everything you have done for me over the years. I will always be grateful. Always. And what about that dashing young man over there. Steve, thank you for making sure everything ran so smoothly today. And finally, I must say a word about the bridesmaids. They were charming and so elegant in everything they did. So please join me in a toast to the bridesmaids.

Ladies and Gentlemen, the bridesmaids!

Model speech 28: Bridegroom's reply

Formal reception or informal wedding party – where the bridegroom has been married before.

Ladies and Gentlemen, thank you so much for attending our wedding and for all these splendid gifts. I would like to offer a few personal thank yous as well. First and foremost, thank you, Anne, for marrying me. This time I am not marrying for better or for worse – I am marrying for good. And thanks to your parents for producing such a beautiful daughter and for arranging this wonderful reception/party. Thanks, too, to my parents – not least for having me. And also to Zack for getting me to the church on time. Finally, my thanks must go to the charming young ladies who did such a great job in helping Anne up the aisle. Please join me in a toast to the bridesmaids.

Ladies and Gentlemen, the bridesmaids!

Model speech 29: Bridegroom's reply

Formal reception or informal wedding party – where both parties have been divorced or widowed at least once.

(You will need to word your speech very carefully, according to whether you and your wife have been widowed and/or divorced, and also how long ago this happened.)

Thank you, James, for those wise words. Joan and I know how lucky we are to have this second chance in life and we have decided to grab it with both hands. In the words of the old song, 'We're not so old, and not so plain, and we're quite prepared to marry again'. Whatever we may have said during the wedding ceremony, we are not marrying for better or worse – we are marrying for good.

My wife and I [*pause*] want to thank you all for coming to our wedding today, and for your lovely gifts. A particular word of thanks is due to James and Joyce for laying on this wonderful reception/party. Next, I must thank Rolf, who was undoubtedly the best man to get me to the church on time. And finally, my thanks go to Ena, Martha and Minnie, those charming young ladies who did such a wonderful job today. Ladies and Gentlemen, will you now all join me in drinking a toast to the bridesmaids?

Ladies and Gentlemen, the bridesmaids!

But what if you already have one or more children? You may decide not to make any reference to this in your speech. However, this could seem a little odd, because the guests are certain to already know about your child(ren). Whatever you decide, make sure all the other speech makers know precisely how you want them to play it so none of them will say anything out of turn. If you do decide to refer to your family, the following is the sort of thing you should say.

Model speech 30: Bridegroom's reply

Formal reception or informal wedding party – where the couple already has at least one child.

Thank you for those kind words. My wife and I [*pause*] are delighted you came to our wedding. As they say, better late than never. You see we needed a new toaster and a few saucepans and as Argos was closed . . .

I'd like to take this opportunity to say a few personal thank yous. First and foremost to Paula for marrying me. To her parents for being such great people and for arranging this wonderful reception/party. To my parents for being the best parents in the world. To Robin for being my best man and my best friend. And finally, to the most charming set of bridesmaids I have ever seen – Rita, Mavis, Vera and our lovely daughter, Jodie. So will you all kindly stand and drink a toast to these delightful bridesmaids.

Ladies and Gentlemen, the bridesmaids!

But perhaps only one of you is already a parent. If you decide not to make any reference to this, make sure nobody else is going to either. However, if you are going to be quite open about it, speeches 31 and 32 should be of help.

Model speech 31: Bridegroom's reply
Formal reception or informal wedding party – where he already has a child.

Ladies and Gentlemen, my wife and I [*pause*] thank you all for your presence – in both senses of the word. I'd like to add a few personal thank yous, too. To Sarah's parents, George and Martha, for laying on this wonderful reception/wedding party and, even more, for producing Sarah. George, thank you for those wise words. I do not deserve the good things you said of me, but I shall try to deserve them, and be worthy of my family – my daughter, Wendy, and her mother, Sarah. Thanks, too, to my parents for being so supportive over the years. You could not have done more. And thank you, Ken, for getting me to the church on time. But my greatest thanks must go to Sarah – for marrying me.

It is my final duty – no, pleasure – to thank the bridesmaids for helping Sarah up the aisle. Don't they look a picture? Will you all join me in drinking a toast to them?

Ladies and Gentlemen, the bridesmaids!

Model speech 32: Bridegroom's reply
Formal reception or informal wedding party – where his wife already has a child.

Ladies and Gentlemen, thank you, Peter, for those wise words. My wife and I [*pause*] would like to thank you all for coming to our wedding and for your most generous gifts. I'd like to take this opportunity to add a few personal thank yous too. Thanks to June's parents, Peter and Sandra, for arranging this wonderful reception/wedding party and, of course, for arranging June. Thanks to my parents, Nick and Sue, for everything they have done for me over the years – far too much for me to even begin to describe here today. Thank you. And thanks to Alan for being the best best man a bridegroom could have hoped for. But most of all, thanks to June for taking me on. I will try my hardest to be a worthy husband and father.

Finally, what can I say about that delightful set of bridesmaids over there? They were magnificent. Please join me in drinking a toast to them.

Ladies and Gentlemen, the bridesmaids!

Model speech 33: Bridegroom's reply
Informal wedding party.

Ladies and Gentlemen – Friends, my wife and I *[pause]* want to say a sincere thank you for coming to our wedding and for being so generous with your presents. And I want to say thank you on my own behalf to Kylie for taking me on, to her parents for producing such a wonderful daughter, to my parents for being so supportive to me over the years, and to my best man, John, who made sure everything ran so smoothly. I have one final duty – no, it is not a duty, it is a genuine pleasure. I have the pleasure of proposing a toast to the health of the young ladies who supported Kylie so magnificently today.

Ladies and Gentlemen, the bridesmaids!

Model speech 34: Bridegroom's reply
Informal wedding party – where the bride's father is recently deceased.

Ladies and Gentlemen, my wife and I *[pause]* are delighted that you found the time to join us here today. It has made such a difference to have been surrounded by our closest friends on this, our big day. We have been overwhelmed by your kindness and generosity. Jenny's mother has been wonderful. We all know what a very difficult time she has been through recently but she insisted on helping with all our preparations and I am sure that her daughter's wedding will have provided a bright light in what must have otherwise been a very dark year for her. Margaret, thank you so much for all your support. I can promise you that you haven't lost a daughter, you've gained a son. They say a girl grows up to be like her mother – well I can only hope it's true.

And I mustn't forget my parents. Their help, like Margaret's, has been above and beyond the call of duty.

Then there is Geraint, my best man. We met at university and I can tell you that those of you who don't know him are the luckiest people in the world – because the pleasure of getting to know him lies ahead of you.

Finally, I must mention the bridesmaids who have done so much to help my wife. Don't they look a picture? Let's all drink a toast to them.

Ladies and Gentlemen, the bridesmaids!

Model speech 35: Bridegroom's reply
Informal wedding party – where one of his parents is recently deceased.

Thank you, Bruce, for those kind words. My wife and I *[pause]* are delighted you could all make it to our wedding today. And thank you so much for your generous gifts. I hope to be able to thank you all person- ally later. Thanks, too, to Alice's mum and dad, Bruce and Rosemary, for allowing me to marry their beautiful daughter and for arranging this magnificent party. And thanks, of course, must also go to my mum who has done so much for me – much more than I could possibly begin to tell you about here. And dad was so much looking forward to today that I agree, Bruce, in a sense he must be celebrating with us. *[Obviously, this was a response to something said in an earlier speech and it was not in his draft.]*

I would also like to thank Desmond for being such an efficient best man. Although I'm not sure how thankful to be because I haven't heard his speech yet.

Finally, thanks to these delightful young ladies who have done a great job in helping Alice up the aisle – although I hope she came to the church of her own free will. So will you all stand and join me in drink- ing a toast to the bridesmaids?

Ladies and Gentlemen, the bridesmaids!

(Where both the bride and bridegroom have recently lost a parent adapt and personalise the relevant parts of speeches 34 and 35.)

Model speech 36: Bridegroom's reply
Informal wedding party – where the bride was brought up in a single- parent family.

Ladies and Gentlemen, you may not realise it but this is a truly historic day. This day, 16th May, will always be remembered because of three world-famous events. The first Oscars were awarded in 1929; singer

Janet Jackson was born in 1966; and on this day in 199-, I married Michelle!

My wife and I *[pause]* want to thank you all for attending this little gathering and for your very useful gifts. I would also like to offer a few personal thank yous. To Beth, my new mother-in-law, for bringing up her daughter to become the charming, witty and considerate lady I was fortunate enough to marry today. To my parents, Jayne and Christopher, for having me – and for much, much more than that. To Branwell for being the best best man a groom could hope for. And to Charlotte, Emily and Ann for being such delightful bridesmaids. In fact, I think we should drink a toast to them, don't you?

Ladies and Gentlemen, the bridesmaids!

Model speech 37: Bridegroom's reply
Informal wedding party – where he was brought up in a single-parent family.

Thank you, Gavin, for those kind words. My wife and I *[pause]* would like to thank you all for attending our wedding and for your most generous gifts and good wishes. If I could also add one or two personal thank yous . . . Thank you to Esther's parents, Gavin and Ruth, for so readily accepting me as one of their family. To my mother, Rebecca, for being the best mum in the world. To Howard for not losing the ring. And to the charming bridesmaids, Isra and Caroline for doing such a magnificent job today. Will you all join me in drinking a toast to them?

Ladies and Gentlemen, the bridesmaids!

(Where both the bride and bridegroom were brought up in single-parent families adapt and personalise the relevant parts of speeches 36 and 37.)

It is not necessary for the bride to make a speech, but if she wants to the number and order of speeches will need to be revised, perhaps to:

1. Toast to the bride and groom by the bride's father.
2. Response by the bridegroom (omitting the toast to the bridesmaids).
3. Response by the bride.
4. Toast to the bridesmaids by a close friend, relative or godfather.
5. Response by the best man.

What follows is the sort of thing the bride should say:

Model speech 38: Bride's response
Formal reception or informal wedding party.

Ladies and Gentlemen, I'm very glad to break with tradition and say a few words of my own on this happy occasion. This is the happiest day in my life since I was in the arms of another woman's husband – my mother's. Mum told me the only time a woman really succeeds in changing a man is when he's a baby – so I still have time to change Shane. He thinks he's going to be boss in the house, when actually he's going to be housing the boss. Thank you all for your generous gifts, thanks to Shane's parents for making me feel I am their daughter, and to my parents for more than I could ever begin to tell. Thank you.

Model speech 39: Bridegroom's reply
Formal reception or informal wedding party – where there are no bridesmaids, but there is a maid/matron of honour.

Ladies and Gentlemen, my wife and I *[pause]* thank you all so much for coming to our wedding and for bringing these wonderful gifts. We would particularly like to thank our parents for all the support they have given us over the years and our mothers in particular for arranging this superb reception/party. Our thanks also must go to Damian, my best man, and to Marlene, Kelly's maid of honour. They were magnificent. In fact, would you join me and drink a toast to Damian and Marlene?

Ladies and Gentlemen, to Damian and Marlene!

Where there are no bridesmaids and no maid/matron of honour, the toast is to your parents-in-law.

Model speech 40: Bridegroom's reply
Formal reception or informal wedding party – where there are no bridesmaids and no maid/matron of honour.

Ladies and Gentlemen, my wife and I *[pause]* are delighted you were able to join us on this, our happiest day. It goes almost without saying what a difference it makes to have our closest friends here with us. Thank you so much for your kind wishes and your wonderful presents. Thanks also to Jayne's parents for making me really feel like one of the family – which of course I now am – and to my parents for everything they have done for me over the years. Finally, my thanks go to Jimmy for not losing the ring.

I cannot begin to tell you how happy Jenny and I are today. I wish the whole world could be feeling the same way and I hope you all enjoy a wonderful afternoon/evening. Please raise your glasses and join me in drinking a toast to our generous hosts, two wonderful people, my new parents-in-law, George and Mildred.

To George and Mildred!

RESPONSE ON BEHALF OF THE BRIDESMAIDS

Rather oddly, it is traditional for the best man to respond to the toast to the bridesmaids. All that is required is acknowledgement of the toast, and a few light-hearted and humorous words about the bridegroom – with a couple of compliments and congratulatory remarks woven in.

While you could also tell a joke or two against yourself, *never* say a single word against the bride or her mother (although a teasing remark about the bride's *job* or *hobby* would not be out of place). A little flippancy is fine, but you must avoid anything that could be considered at all risqué, offensive or cynical. Also steer well clear of any emotional or serious issues – such weighty matters are the prerogative of the bride's father and the bridegroom.

Don't just string a series of jokes together either – you are not a stand-up comedian. Your overall purpose is to respond to the toast to the bridesmaids and to return a few sincere congratulatory remarks to the happy couple. The best way to do this in an amusing and entertaining manner is to sugar some teasing remarks with a few sincere words of praise and compliments.

Because this is a very jokey, upbeat speech, the backgrounds and circumstances of the bride and bridegroom (from a single-parent family; parent recently deceased; married before, and so on) are largely irrelevant, although obviously you must take care to avoid saying anything insensitive. For example, if the groom's father died of a coronary, don't say he had a heart of gold.

If you are the final speaker, signal this by reading the tele-messages immediately after finishing your speech (having first checked that they are not X-rated). If there are to be more speeches (see speeches 49 and 50), stand up, pointedly look at the clock, and read the messages after the final speaker to ensure he really *is* the final speaker.

Try to keep the tele-message session interesting by giving a few background details about the contents of the messages and about the people who sent them. Crack a joke if the moment seems right. As always, aim to end on a particularly high note. You could end with the funniest or most emotional message, or with one from some relatives who live on the other side of the world, or perhaps with one from some very old family friends (in both senses of the word). Alternatively, you could simply *make up* the last message. However, if you do this, you must make it obvious to everyone that this is a joke: 'And finally, this is from the writer who created *Jeeves and Wooster* – P.G. Woodhouse. It says, '''All unhappy marriages are a result of the husband having brains''. I have total confidence this marriage will be an exceptionally happy one.'

Model speech 41: Best man's reply
Formal reception – Example 1.

Ladies and Gentlemen, thank you, Kevin, for those kind words about the bridesmaids and attendants. It has been a pleasure for all of us to be a small part of your big day. And what about the dresses chosen by Sally and her mother Denise? They have attracted so much favourable comment from the guests here that I have to give them a special mention. *[Pause for cries of 'Here, here'.] [This reference to their dresses obviously was not in his draft speech.]*

Before I say a word or two about our groom, I must admit that I have made a very similar little speech about Kevin twice before – once to the Ashford's Arsonists' Association and once to the Clitheroe's Clog-dancers Club. So I apologise to those of you who may have already heard it once before. And to those of you who have already heard it twice, please don't burn my shoes.

As Max Bygraves used to say, I wanna tell you a story, because I think it sums up nicely the kind of man Sally has married. Soon after we met, Kevin invited me to his eighteenth birthday party. At the time I knew hardly anyone in Manchester – in fact I was getting a bit depressed with life. Kevin didn't really know me either – I was an acquaintance of a friend of a friend. But despite this he absolutely insisted I came to his do. He wouldn't take no for an answer and he almost forced details of his address upon me. For the first time since I moved here, I felt wanted.

He said, 'A number 23 bus will bring you right to my door – 9 Rosamond Street. Walk up to the front door and press the doorbell with your elbow.' 'Why my elbow, Kev?' I asked. 'Because you'll have a bottle of wine under one arm, a box of chocolates under the other, a four-pack in one hand and my pressie in the other, won't you?' he replied. Yes, Sally, that's the kind of man you've married.

Have you noticed how few single people were invited here today? That was Kevin's idea as well. He's not stupid, despite rumours to the contrary. He told me that if he invited only married people all the presents would be clear profit. But in all honesty, Kevin doesn't know the meaning of the word meanness. Mind you he doesn't know the meaning of lots of other words either.

Talking of the meaning of words, do you know what the name Kevin actually means? Well, believe it or not, it comes from the Celtic word for handsome. Ridiculous isn't it? On the other hand, the name Sally means princess and who could argue with that?

When I asked Kevin about today's wedding arrangements, he said, 'Oh, I'll leave all that to you. But I do want Bells, and get at least a dozen bottles.' Well I don't know about Bells, but I work with Kevin at Fenn Street School and I can tell you he is one of the best Teachers I know.

Kevin, you are a very lucky man to have married Sally – but then again Sally, you are an equally lucky lady to have married Kevin, and on behalf of the bridesmaids, I wish you both love and happiness!

Now I believe there have been one or two tele-messages. . .

Model speech 42: Best man's reply
Formal reception – Example 2.

Ladies and Gentlemen, thank you, John, for those kind words about the bridesmaids. Personally, though, I would have gone even further. They are the most delightful set of bridesmaids I have ever seen. Be honest,

today you are blinkered and you only have eyes for Janet – and who can blame you?

As Henry VIII said to each of his wives in turn, 'I shall not keep you long.' The reason for this is quite simple: I'm now supposed to sing the bridegroom's praises and tell you all about his good points. Unfortunately, I can't sing, and I can't think of any good points to tell you about – but I shall try.

What can I say about John that has not already been said in crown court? There is nothing I wouldn't do for him and I know there is nothing he wouldn't do for me. In fact, we spend our lives doing nothing for each other.

But I must be very careful what I say about a dentist because one day I could find myself a captive audience in his chair, staring up at the ceiling – and I've seen *Marathon Man*. Last week I arranged to meet him after work at his surgery. I'd had trouble with the car and he said he'd take a look at it. I was a bit early so I glanced through the magazines and newspapers he provides for his patients in the waiting room. Wasn't it terrible about the *Titanic*? He did a great job on the car – but later it cost me £200 to have it overhauled. I was speeding down the M4 when a police car overhauled it.

That's one thing no one can accuse John of – speeding. Everything he does is calm and measured and he will never take any short-cuts. I remember at school we all had to count the traffic going past the main gate. Once Old Chalky – Mr White, our form teacher – had gone, we all went off and played soccer – all but John, of course, who spent the whole afternoon – yes, counting cars. The rest of us agreed we'd all report roughly the same number of cars, lorries and motor bikes to Old Chalky, so John got told off because all his answers were miles out from everybody else's.

But, looking back on it, that afternoon demonstrated how reliable and single-minded he is. It also shows he won't take the easy way out by going along with the crowd when he knows the crowd is wrong – or maybe it showed he doesn't like soccer. What it definitely did show was that he possessed something every aspiring dentist needs – patience, in both sense of the word. And today, John, your patience has been rewarded.

I can't understand why Janet chose you rather than me. But I suppose that it proves men have better taste than women. After all, John chose Janet, but Janet chose John. So now I come to my final wedding day duty which isn't a duty really – it's a real pleasure: on behalf of the bridesmaids and myself I sincerely wish you and your lovely wife, Janet, everlasting love and happiness!

Model speech 43: Best man's reply
Formal reception –Example 3.

Ladies and Gentlemen, I've been best man once before. I think it went OK last time – the couple in question are at least still talking to me. Unfortunately, they're not actually talking to each other. I thought Ruth knew Mark had slept with her younger sister before I mentioned it in my speech – but perhaps the fact he'd slept with her mother came as a surprise.

On such an illustrious day as this it seems odd for me to be called best man. After all, who pays attention to a man in my position today? They all say, 'Doesn't the bride look radiant?' – which she does, and 'What a charming set of bridesmaids' – which they are, and 'What a dashing bridegroom' – which he isn't. But who says, 'What a fine figure of a man the best man is' – which, so very obviously, he is. No, if they notice me at all, they think I'm a waiter or a chauffeur. One lady, who shall remain nameless, even asked if my name was Brad and had I been sent to meet her by the Lonely Hearts Club Escort Agency. But enough of my troubles.

When I made my other wedding speech a man fell asleep. I asked a pageboy to wake him and do you know what the little horror replied? He said, 'You wake him. You were the one who put him to sleep.' Well, today, to make sure I don't make the same mistake again, I promise to be brief.

You know, this really is a truly historic day! This day, 21st July, will always be associated with three of the great events of the twentieth century. Funnyman Robin Williams was born in 1952; Neil Armstrong took a giant step for mankind in 1969; and on this day in 199-, William married Mary. So in 1969 it was Neil Armstrong, but today it is William who is over the moon.

We all know he likes a bit of a flutter and he told me he once dreamt he won eight million on the lottery. 'What would you do about all the begging letters if you ever did win that much?' I asked. 'Oh, I'd still keep sending them,' he replied. Well, today, William, you are not dreaming, and I can tell you you really have hit the jackpot. On behalf of the bridesmaids and myself I wish you both love and everlasting happiness!

Model speech 44: Best man's reply
Informal wedding party – Example 1.

Thank you for those kind words. The bridesmaids and I have really enjoyed this wonderful occasion. Layla said she wanted a simple wedding – and that's exactly what she got – starting with the groom. He is the most independent salesman I know – I can't remember the last time he took an order from anyone. He is also an avid book collector. Last week he complained to me that he had so many that he did not know what to do with them. I suggested he tried reading them. He must spend a lot of money on books, but I think things are going to change. As Layla walked up the aisle, and approached the altar, and sang a hymn, I heard her whisper to her dad, 'Aisle – altar – hymn.' Dougal, you have been warned. Now before I take a pew, on behalf of the bridesmaids, Layla and Dougal, I wish you peace and harmony!

Model speech 45: Best man's reply
Informal wedding party – Example 2.

On behalf of all the attendants, I'd like to thank you sincerely for those kind words. It has been a pleasure for us to have been a small part of your big day. They say that marriage is a process whereby the grocer acquires the account that used to be held by the florist. Well if that's true you won't find Reg complaining because, as you all know, Reg is a grocer. He tells me times are hard – you have to offer bargains to keep your customers. Have you seen the sign in his window? It says, 'Eggs still twelve a dozen.' What a bargain. Well we're all delighted that Reg has decided to put all his eggs in one basket by marrying Maureen. He couldn't have made a better choice. And, as sure as eggs is eggs, they can look forward to – dare I say it? – an eggcellent future together. On behalf of the bridesmaids, Maureen and Reg, I wish you everlasting love and happiness!

Model speech 46: Chief bridesmaid's reply
Formal reception or informal wedding party – where the best man does not respond to the toast or, more unusually, where the chief bridesmaid does as well.

Thank you so much for those kind words. I know I also speak for my fellow bridesmaids when I say it has been a real pleasure for us all today. I have known Louise since she joined us at Blackwall eight years ago. Someone had told her to go to blazes so she decided to become a firefighter. I haven't known Alex for quite so long. He works for BR, but no one is perfect. I suppose he should have been the one carrying

Louise's train today, not us. I told him I had to get home tonight and I asked him the time of the late train to London. 'Take the 10.15,' he suggested, 'that's usually as late as any.'

But enough of this banter. They say marriage is founded on mutual respect. If that is so then this marriage cannot fail. I know how much Alex respects Louise and Louise has told me her pet name for him, which could hardly be more respectful. She told me that as they sit before an open fire on a cold and damp February evening, and as yet another log is needed, she will turn lovingly to her beloved and say, 'Alexander – the grate'. Well, Alexander and Louise, we hope and pray that the future is great for you both and on behalf of myself and the other bridesmaids, I wish you everlasting love and happiness!

Model speech 47: Best man's reply
Formal reception or informal wedding party – where there are no bridesmaids, but there is a maid/matron of honour.

Thank you so much for those kind words. No one knows better than me how much the maid/matron of honour, Marlene, deserves your compliments and thanks. But for Marlene and me it has been a pleasure, not a duty, to have been a small part of your big day. We merely had the enjoyable tasks of assisting and helping to carry out the design and plan for this wedding so ably arranged by Kelly's parents, Frank and Kim. Not only that, they are such charming hosts and wonderful people that I am sure that everyone present here will want to stand and join Marlene and me in proposing a toast to Frank and Kim.

To Frank and Kim!

Model speech 48: Best man's reply
Formal reception or informal reception – where there are no bridesmaids.

Ladies and Gentlemen, the last time I made a wedding speech someone at the back shouted, 'I can't hear you!, – and a man sitting next to me yelled back, 'I'll change places with you!' [*pause*]. In order to avoid any possible musical chairs here today, I intend to speak up and then to shut up.

I have been a best man at many weddings and I admitted to Christopher that my track record has not been that brilliant: 'Could do better', as they used to write on our school reports. In my time I have lost the ring, gone to the wrong church and lost the honeymoon luggage. But did Chris care about these not-so-rare examples of mal-administration? He did not. 'Don't worry,' he said, 'you won't have to do a thing. Just leave it all to Jayne's mum.' And he was right. Mildred, ably assisted by her husband George, really came up trumps. [*If possible, refer to some particularly outstanding feature, such as the beautiful flower arrangements or the magnificent buffet.*] They have created the perfect day – one we shall all remember. So I ask you to raise your glasses and to drink a toast to our friends – Jayne's parents and Christopher's new in-laws, George and Mildred.

To George and Mildred!

If there are no bridesmaids, the bridegroom may not require a speech by the best man (such as speeches 47 and 48). Instead, he might prefer this arrangement:

1. Toast to the couple by a close family friend or relative.
2. Response by the bridegroom.
3. Response by the bride's father.

The first speech could be similar to speech 2 or 15, according to whether you are at a formal reception or informal wedding party. The second could be similar to any of the speeches suitable for the bridegroom and the third similar to any of those suitable for the bride's father, although neither would propose a toast.

It is not uncommon for other guests to speak after the best man (or chief bridesmaid or bridesmaid's father). However, the danger is that too many people will try to get on the bandwaggon, especially after the fire water has flowed liberally. If there are to be any speeches after the reply on behalf of the bridesmaids, it is best to keep other contributions to a minimum, possibly as follows:

1. Toast to the hosts by a close friend or relative of the bridegroom.
2. Reply by the bride's father.
3. The best man reads the tele-messages.

Model speech 49: Close friend or relative of bridegroom's toast of thanks to the host and hostess

Ladies and Gentlemen, what a wonderful day this has been. Everything has run so smoothly from the word go. And who do we have to thank for that? Steve was such a fine and efficient best man and the bridesmaids added so much to the occasion. But our greatest thanks must go to our hosts, Christina's parents and Paul's new in-laws, Margaret and Denis. After all, they organised this event and frankly I don't think it could have been bettered. [*If possible, mention some particularly outstanding aspect of the day – flower arrangements, food, music, dancing or whatever.*] I am sure everyone present will want to stand and join me as I propose a toast to our magnificent hosts, Margaret and Denis.

Ladies and Gentlemen, Margaret and Denis!

Model speech 50: Bride's father's reply to the toast

A longer reply, similar to one of speeches 1–21, but without the toast, is acceptable if he has not spoken before.

Thank you, Nigel, for those most generous words. I'm only going to speak for a moment or two because of my throat – if I go on any longer than that Margaret has threatened to cut it. Of course, it was an absolute pleasure for us to do our bit to help make the day the success it has so clearly been. But the greatest credit must go to you all for making it such a joyous occasion. You have been fantastic. And I hope you will all continue to have a wonderful time this afternoon/evening!

Further Reading

WEDDINGS – GENERAL

The Good Wedding Guide, Sue Carpenter (Equation).
Getting Married, Sarah Caisley (Mason).
Getting Married, Mary Gostelow (Batsford).
The Bridal Path, Eve Anderson (Foulsham).
The Complete Wedding Book, Jill Thomas (World's Work).
The Wedding Day Book, Sue Dobson (Arrow).

PLANNING A WEDDING

How to Plan a Wedding, Mary Kilborn (How To Books).
Planning Your Wedding, Joyce Robins (Hamlyn).
The Step-by-Step Wedding Planner, Eve Anderson (Foulsham).
The Wedding Planner, Angela Lansbury (Ward Lock).
The Complete Wedding Planner, Gail Lawther (Harper Collins).

WEDDING ETIQUETTE

Wedding Etiquette, Patricia and William Derraugh (Foulsham).
Wedding Etiquette, Angela Lansbury (Ward Lock).
Wedding Etiquette Properly Explained, Vernon Heaton (Elliot Right Way Books).
The Complete Guide to Wedding Etiquette, Margot Lawrence (Ward Lock).

THE MAIN PLAYERS

The Bride's Book, Drusilla Beyfus (Allen Lane).
The Bridegroom's Handbook, Sean Callery (Ward Lock).

The Best Man's Handbook, Henry Russell (David and Charles).
How to be the Best Man, Angela Lansbury (Ward Lock).
How to be a Bridesmaid, Angela Lansbury (Ward Lock).

SECOND WEDDINGS

Emily Post on Second Weddings, Emily Post (Harper Perennial).

PUBLIC SPEAKING

Just Say A Few Words, Bob Monkhouse (Lennard Publishing).
How to Master Public Speaking, Anne Nicholls (How To Books).
The Complete Public Speaker, Gyles Brandreth MP (Robert Hale).
Janner's Complete Speechmaker, Greville Janner QC MP (Business Books).
Debrett's Guide to Speaking in Public, Carole McKenzie (Headline).

ANNIVERSARIES

Today's the Day, Jeremy Beadle (W.H. Allen).
The Amazing Almanac, Gyles Brandreth MP (Pelham Books).
The Book of Days, Anthony Frewin (Collins).
The Anniversary Book, Christopher Downing (Futura).
Hamlyn Dictionary of Dates and Anniversaries (Hamlyn).
Chambers' Dates (Chambers).
On This Day: The History of the World in 366 Days, Sian Facer, Editor (Hamlyn).

QUOTATIONS

The library shelves are weighed down with these books. I find the following particularly useful:

The Oxford Book of Quotations (OUP).
Stevenson's Book of Quotations (Cassell).
The Penguin Dictionary of Humorous Quotations, Fred Metcalf (Viking).
Cassell's Book of Humorous Quotations (Cassell).
The New Penguin Dictionary of Quotations (Viking).
A Dictionary of Twentieth Century Quotations, Nigel Rees (Fontana).

A Dictionary of Contemporary Quotations (David and Charles).
The Oxford Dictionary of Modern Quotations (OUP).
Apt and Amusing Quotations, G.F. Lamb (Elliot Right Way Books).

NAMES

The Guinness Book of Names, Leslie Dunkling (Guinness Superlatives).
Everyman's Dictionary of First Names, Leslie Dunkling and William
    Gosling (J.M. Dent).
Bloomsbury Dictionary of First Names, Julia Cresswell (Bloomsbury).
The Concise Dictionary of English Christian Names, E.G. Withycombe,
    (Omega).
A Dictionary of First Names, Patrick Hanks and Flavia Hodges
    (Oxford).
Islamic Names, Annemarie Schimmel (Edinburgh University Press).
A Dictionary of Hindu Names, Ramesh and Urmilla Dogra (Aditya
    Prakashan).
The Book of Surnames, Peter Verstappen (Pelham Books).
The Penguin Dictionary of Surnames, Basil Cottle (Allen Lane).

ANECDOTES AND JOKES

There are hundreds – perhaps thousands – of these books. Here is a
personal selection:

The Faber Book of Anecdotes, Clifton Fadiman (Faber).
Jokes and Quotes for Speeches, Peter Eldin (Ward Lock).
The Right Joke for the Right Occasion, Kevin Goldstein-Jackson (Elliot
    Right Way Books).
1497 Jokes, Stories and Anecdotes, Herbert V. Prochnow (Sterling).
3500 Good Jokes for Speakers, Gerald Lieberman (Thorsons).
5000 One- and Two-Line Jokes, Leopold Fechter (Thorsons).

Index

How to Sell Your Business
Robert Ziman

Are you thinking of selling your business? Perhaps you feel it is time for a change, or retirement beckons, or your personal circumstances have changed. Whatever the reasons, you will certainly want to get the best deal. But how do you market a business? What about the timing, method and costs? What about confidentiality, and negotiating with prospective buyers? Written by a business transfer agent with a lifetime's experience, this book shows you step-by-step how to manage the whole process from the beginning, through setbacks, and towards a satisfactory outcome. It is complete with many examples, checklists, sample documents and other essential information to set you on your way.

160pp illus. 1 85703 119 9.

How to Invest in Stocks and Shares
Dr John White (2nd edition)

This book has been specially updated to help and guide those with a lump sum or surplus income to invest and who are considering investing all or part of this in quoted securities. Dr John White, an Oxford graduate, is himself an experienced investor and adviser to an investment company. He has a professional background in computers and has produced a range of software for chart analysis. 'User friendly . . . Contains many practical examples and illustrations of typical share-dealing documents. There are also case studies which give you a feel for your own inclinations about risk versus profit . . . Demystifies the world of stocks and shares.' *OwnBase.* 'Will be a help to private investors . . . Gives an easy to understand guide to the way the stockmarket works, and how the investor should go about setting up a suitable investment strategy.' *What Investment.*

208pp illus. 1 85703 112 1.

How to Retire Abroad
Roger Jones

Increasing numbers of people are looking for opportunities to base their retirement overseas — away from many of the hassles of life in the UK. This book meets the need for a really comprehensive and practical guide to retiring abroad — from the initial planning stages, to choosing the right location and property, and adapting to a completely new environment. Such a big change in lifestyle can involve many pitfalls. Written by a specialist in expatriate matters, this handbook will guide you successfully step-by-step through the whole process of finding a new home, coping with key matters such as tax, foreign investment, property, health care, and even working overseas. The book is complete with a country-by-country guide. Roger Jones is a freelance author specialising in expatriate information. His other books include *How to Get a Job Abroad, How to Teach Abroad* and *How to Get a Job in America.*

176pp. 1 85703 051 6.